150 Gems of Irish Music
for Flute

by Grey Larsen

www.melbay.com/98216BCDEB

© 2013 BY MEL BAY PUBLICATIONS, INC., PACIFIC, MO 63069.
ALL RIGHTS RESERVED. INTERNATIONAL COPYRIGHT SECURED. B.M.I. MADE AND PRINTED IN U.S.A.
No part of this publication may be reproduced in whole or in part, or stored in a retrieval system, or transmitted in any form
or by any means, electronic, mechanical, photocopy, recording, or otherwise, without written permission of the publisher.

Visit us on the Web at www.melbay.com — E-mail us at email@melbay.com

Table of Contents

Dedication 3
Acknowledgments and Credits 4
Introduction 5
   Chapter One: Ornamentation and Its Notation 12
   Chapter Two: Modes and Other Notation Matters 27
   Chapter Three: Breathing and Phrasing 33
SECTION ONE: Flute-Friendly Tunes 47
      Jigs 48
      Reels 60
      Hornpipes 73
      Other Tune Types 77
SECTION TWO: Tunes of Non-Wind Origin 83
      Jigs 84
      Reels 88
      Hornpipes 93
      Other Tune Types 95
SECTION THREE: Tunes Requiring the Use of Keys 99
      Jigs 100
      Reels 104
      Hornpipes 108
      Other Tune Types 110
   Appendix: Playing Tunes on Non-D Flutes 112
   Contents of the Companion Audio 124
   Index of Tune Titles 126
   Index of Tunes by Tune Type 127
   Index of Tune Sources 128
   About the Author 129
   Books and Recordings by Grey Larsen 129

The Irish Flute and the Modern Flute

The wooden Irish flute (keyless or keyed) uses a basic "simple-system"[1] fingering that is identical to that of the tin whistle and is very closely related to that of the uilleann pipes, the bellows-blown bagpipe of Ireland. No doubt this has helped make the simple-system flute a natural choice for traditional Irish musicians. Since all three are simple-system instruments, their fingering and ornamentation techniques are readily adaptable to one another. There is a great deal of overlap among players of these three instruments.

While the six primary holes of the simple-system flute are covered only by fingers, many of these flutes have supplementary metal keys to open and close additional holes and make it more practical to play the notes E♭, F♮, G♯ and B♭. These keys (there are typically one, four, six, or eight of them) may also extend the range of the instrument down to low C♯, C♮ or B.

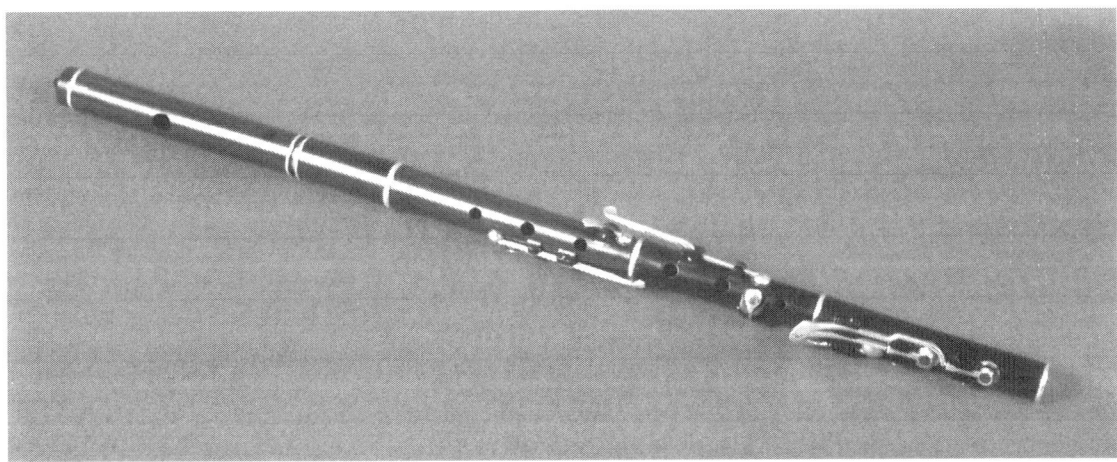

Figure 1. An eight-key wooden flute in cocuswood and silver by Rudall and Rose, serial # 4973, made in London in 1844. English flutes of this period have been highly prized by players of Irish flute music. Today's makers of Irish flutes often base their designs on such 19th century instruments.

While the wooden Irish flute is favored by nearly all Irish flute players, it is possible to play Irish music very well on modern flutes, as evidenced by such great recent and contemporary players as Paddy Carty of Co. Galway, Paddy Taylor of Co. Limerick, Noel Rice of Co. Tipperary, and Irish-American flutist Joanie Madden of New York, a member of the group *Cherish the Ladies*.

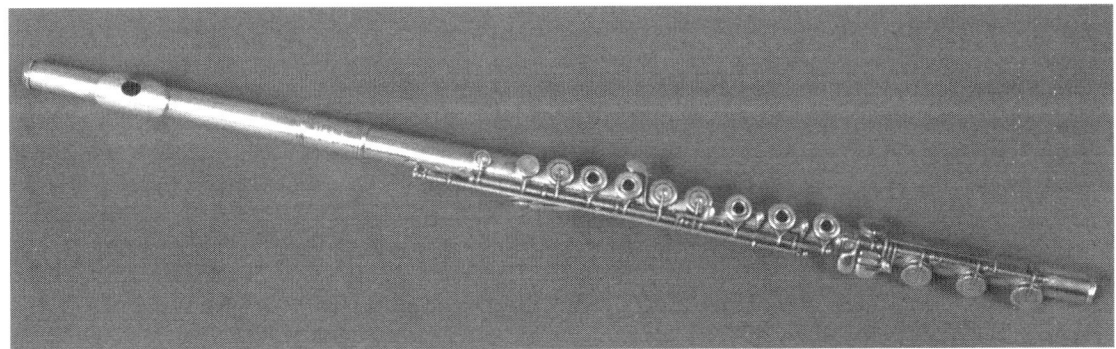

Figure 2. A silver Boehm-system flute made in 1978 by the William Haynes Company of Boston, serial # 44166.

There is much more information on flutes and the history of flute playing in Ireland in *The Essential Guide to Irish Flute and Tin Whistle*. (See "Two Additional Resources" on p. 10.)

---

[1] Simple-system flutes (and whistles) have six primary tone holes that are covered and uncovered solely by the fingers, with no mechanical keywork intervening between the fingers and these holes. Covering all six of these holes on a simple-system flute in the key of D yields a low D note. Uncovering them one by one, from low to high, results in an ascending scale in the D Ionian mode (i.e., the D major scale).

Ornamentation and Breathing Suggestions

The tune transcriptions in this collection include my suggestions for ornamentation and creating appropriate breathing spaces. For those of you not yet fluent in traditional Irish music, these suggestions may help you achieve the experience of playing in a fully-realized traditional manner, and provide a reference point in the evolution of your own personal style. Experienced players may find fresh ornamentation and phrasing ideas in these transcriptions as well.

To make the best use of the transcriptions you'll need to understand the ornamentation and breathing symbols I use, and how I use them. For this and much more, see "Chapter One: Ornamentation and Its Notation" on pp. 12-26 and "Chapter Three: Breathing and Phrasing" on pp. 33-44.

My ornamentation style, and hence my suggestions, tend more toward the spare and lean than the dense and florid. I hope this relative frugality will help make the music accessible and leave room for your own exploration. If you wish to have the transcriptions without suggested ornamentation and breathing places, see "'Blank Slate' Transcriptions - *300 Gems of Irish Music for All Instruments*" on p. 10.

Due to the space limitations of this collection I can offer only one example of how one might ornament and phrase each tune. The book/CD set *Down the Back Lane: Variation in Traditional Irish Dance Music* provides transcriptions and recordings of tunes being varied over the course of three repetitions. For more information, see p. 10.

Transcriptions Are Only Snapshots

For many of us, a tune neatly written in music notation carries an unspoken message: "*This* is the way to play the tune." That presumption, whatever its source, is wrong and needs to be discarded.

There is no such thing as a definitive version, or setting, of a traditional Irish tune. The music is by nature personal, and variable through small-scale improvisation. So please do ***not*** give my transcriptions too much authority! There are many variants of these tunes, and many right ways to ornament and phrase them.

I invite you to regard all Irish tune transcriptions merely as snapshots of moving, living, changing entities. Like a photograph, a transcription captures only a slice of time and represents only one of many possible points of view. When you hear these tunes played by others, you will notice many differences between their versions and the ones in this collection. That diversity is a cherished part of the tradition.

How does one learn to spontaneously vary a tune in appropriate ways? By listening to the playing of experienced musicians over a long period of time. Through such committed immersion in the music we gradually absorb the knowledge and insight that enable us to extemporize in ways that are both culturally appropriate and expressive of our individuality.

Tune Sources

At the upper right of many of the transcriptions you will find information about the source upon which I based my version. Some of these tunes I learned from my earliest mentors: Co. Galway melodeon player Michael J. Kennedy (1900-1978), Co. Sligo flute player Tom Byrne (1920-2001) and Co. Leitrim fiddler Tom McCaffrey (1916-2006). Other tunes I learned from commercial or field recordings of great players made in the 20th and early 21st centuries.

I am not presenting exact, literal documents of how these musicians played (most of them are not, or were not, flute players), but have adapted their versions to the flute while trying to remain faithful to the essence of their interpretations. In some cases, I have altered a few of their notes in order to bring a tune setting a little closer to how I hear the tune being played in sessions and on contemporary recordings.

When no source information is shown, it is most often because I have learned the tune from a variety of musicians and have evolved my own version over the years.

The Companion CDs

Despite the fact that these transcriptions include ornamentation and breathing suggestions, music notation can never fully convey the richness of traditional music. The companion CDs are therefore an essential component of this collection. Below each tune transcription you'll find a reference to its corresponding CD location.

On these CDs I play all 150 tunes, one time through, on Irish flute. When I take a breath, it is in accord with each tune's notated breathing suggestions. The ornamentation shown in the transcriptions is accurately reflected in the recordings for the first time through each part of the tune. During the repetition of any part, the ornamentation heard may vary in small ways from what is written.

Tunes 1 through 94 (the flute-friendly tunes) appear on CD #1. Tunes 95 through 150, as well as the tunes from the Appendix, appear on CD #2. Recordings of some of the musical examples from pp. 16-43 are also found on CD #2, just before the tunes from the Appendix. See pp. 124-125 for a list of the contents of the two discs.

When learning tunes from the recordings, you may find it helpful to slow them down. You can do so with various software programs and hardware devices.

LET YOUR EAR LEAD THE WAY

Before you start to play from a tune transcription, I encourage you first to listen repeatedly to its recording and learn it by ear, or at least to become familiar with the melody that way, learning to hum or sing it as best you can. The notation is best used as a supplement to learning these tunes by ear, or as a reminder of tunes you have already begun to learn. You will find that there are subtle aspects of the music that cannot be written down and can only be experienced through listening.

I believe that everyone can learn by ear. We all did so when, as young children, we learned the common songs that we heard all around us. Though many of us have grown more or less distant from the natural aural learning of our childhoods, I am convinced that the ability to learn by ear is still in us, ready to be reinvigorated. The more you come to trust and rely upon your ear again, the more direct, visceral, and satisfying your experience of music will become. This may take time and patience, but both the process and the results are very rewarding.

If you believe that you must use written music to learn tunes, I invite you to gently set that belief aside – you can always have it back – and allow yourself to start reclaiming a more natural mode of learning Irish music. Try starting small by working with just one short phrase at a time. Please be patient. Allow yourself time to explore and make mistakes abundantly. Mistakes are not bad things! Quite the contrary. They are essential steps in the process of feeling your way around inside a tune. Pay attention to the guidance that so-called mistakes provide you, and have faith that, given time, patience and trust, your musical ear will increasingly rise to the occasion.

For more discussion of learning by ear, see *The Essential Guide to Irish Flute and Tin Whistle* or *The Essential Tin Whistle Toolbox*. (For details on these two books, see "Two Additional Resources" on p. 10.)

MUSIC READING SKILLS

If you are learning to read music or wish to improve your music reading skills, this book and its recordings might well be helpful. The meaning of the music notation will likely become more apparent if you first learn a tune by ear and then examine its transcription.

A COMPANION COLLECTION: *150 GEMS OF IRISH MUSIC FOR TIN WHISTLE*

150 Gems of Irish Music for Tin Whistle is a companion to this collection. As with the present book, its tunes include ornamentation and breathing suggestions.

Although customized for tin whistle players, almost all of its tunes are easily played on the keyless Irish flute. All of its tunes can be played on the keyed Irish flute and the modern flute.

These two books share no common tunes, but they have a similar structure.

Here's the main difference between them: in place of this book's third section (which contains 28 tunes that require the use of keys) the whistle book features 28 tunes that are best played on non-D whistles, along with instructions on how to finger them. If players have whistles in C, A, G, E and F, in addition to a D, they can play a great many tunes in Irish sessions that they could not otherwise play on whistle, including tunes in modes such as D Dorian and Aeolian, G Dorian and Aeolian, and C, F and A Ionian. (For an exploration of modes, see "Chapter Two: Modes and Other Notation Matters" on pp. 27-32.)

There are also quite a few tunes which, while they can be played on a D whistle, sound as good or better, I feel, when played on a lower-pitched whistle, especially a low A or G. (I often bring these two whistles to sessions and enjoy discovering tunes that work well on them.) *150 Gems of Irish Music for Tin Whistle* includes a selection of such tunes, along with instructions on how to finger them. This represents a use of low A, G and F whistles that, to the best of my knowledge, has not been explored before in tune collections.

Both Collections Are Suitable for Other Melodic Instruments

Most of the 300 tunes in these two collections are quite well-suited to all three wind instruments of the Irish tradition: flute, tin whistle and uilleann pipes. The suggestions for ornamentation work equally well for all three, and the breathing suggestions are appropriate for both flute and tin whistle.

Even though pipers do not need to create breathing spaces in a tune, they may enjoy considering the breathing suggestions as places where they too can omit or shorten notes, thereby perhaps discovering some new approaches to phrasing. Players of fiddle, accordion, concertina, tenor banjo, mandolin, harp, and other melody instruments might enjoy using this collection in a similar way.

While not all the ornamentation suggestions transfer easily to string and free reed instruments, many of them do, and trying them out may help players of non-wind instruments explore their own approaches to ornamentation.

"Blank Slate" Transcriptions - *300 Gems of Irish Music for All Instruments*

For those who wish to have copies of these tunes *without* ornamentation and breathing suggestions, the book *300 Gems of Irish Music for All Instruments*[2] combines into one volume such "blank slate" versions of the tunes from both of the *150 Gems* collections.

These tune settings leave low notes (below the flute's low D) in their original register, making the transcriptions more useful to players whose instruments have such low notes. This also makes it easier for wind players to make their own decisions about how to accommodate notes that fall below their instrument's range.

Down the Back Lane: Variation in Traditional Irish Dance Music

Since the suggestions shown in the *150 Gems* books represent only one out of many ways a player might spontaneously ornament and phrase a tune, I have made a supplementary collection of tune transcriptions and recordings, entitled *Down the Back Lane: Variation in Traditional Irish Dance Music,*[3] in which I present transcriptions and recordings of several of the tunes found in the *150 Gems* collections. In *Down the Back Lane,* each tune is played three times through (instead of once). Each repetition of a tune is notated independently, showing complete details of how one repetition differs from the others with respect to ornamentation, breathing, slurring and tonguing, vibrato and melodic variation.

I hope these examples will reinforce the fact that traditional Irish tunes are always changing and that there is no such thing as a definitive setting of a tune.

Two Additional Resources

If you wish to explore Irish flute and tin whistle playing in more depth, you'll find a wealth of information in my 480-page book and two-CD package, *The Essential Guide to Irish Flute and Tin Whistle*[4]. At the time of this writing, it is the most comprehensive work of its kind. Written for beginning to advanced players, it includes a thorough orientation to traditional Irish music, guidance on holding and blowing the instruments, in-depth examinations of ornamentation, breathing, phrasing and melodic variation, systematic exercises for the practice of ornamentation, and 27 meticulously-detailed transcriptions of recordings from great whistle and flute players dating from 1925 to 2001.

Players of the modern, Boehm-system flute may wish to consult its Appendix B for information and advice on fingering choices and adapting traditional ornamentation techniques to their instrument.

The Essential Tin Whistle Toolbox[5] is a slimmer volume that takes the player from the beginner through the intermediate stage of Irish tin whistle playing. Based upon material presented in *The Essential Guide to Irish Flute and Tin Whistle,* the smaller book includes a chapter for beginning whistle players not found in the larger one.

For information on all my books, and to download free excerpts, please visit www.greylarsen.com.

---

[2] Grey Larsen, *300 Gems of Irish Music for All Instruments* (Pacific, Missouri: Mel Bay Publications, Inc., 2013).
[3] Grey Larsen, *Down the Back Lane: Variation in Traditional Irish Dance Music* (Pacific, Missouri: Mel Bay Publications, Inc., 2013).
[4] Grey Larsen, *The Essential Guide to Irish Flute and Tin Whistle* (Pacific, Missouri: Mel Bay Publications, Inc., 2003).
[5] Grey Larsen, *The Essential Tin Whistle Toolbox* (Pacific, Missouri: Mel Bay Publications, Inc., 2004).

Alternate Tune Titles

Many traditional Irish tunes have multiple names. In all of these collections I have listed only one title per tune, but an online search will often yield quite a few alternates.

While most tunes are widely known by English titles, some are more commonly known by titles in the Irish language. In these cases, I give the Irish title first, followed by an English translation. Titles in both languages are then listed in "Contents of the Companion CDs" on pp. 124-125 and in the indices on pp. 126-127.

Gender Convention

In this book I have decided to avoid the cumbersome use of both genders for the personal pronoun. Instead of writing *he or she, his or her,* etc., I use the feminine gender. In this way I can contribute to correcting the imbalance caused by centuries of books which contain only masculine forms.

An Apology for Some Confusion

When this book and its companion volume were first envisioned, they were given the working titles *Celtic Encyclopedia for Tin Whistle* and *Celtic Encyclopedia for Flute.* Unfortunately, these titles were mentioned in several printings of *The Essential Guide to Irish Flute and Tin Whistle* and *The Essential Tin Whistle Toolbox.* I apologize for any confusion this may have caused.

Chapter One: Ornamentation and Its Notation

With the publication of *The Essential Guide to Irish Flute and Tin Whistle* in 2003, I proposed a new system of understanding and notating Irish flute and tin whistle ornamentation. In the following pages I'll discuss only the elements of that system that are necessary for making good use of the tune transcriptions in this book. For a far deeper exploration of the subject, please refer to *The Essential Guide to Irish Flute and Tin Whistle*.

What Is Ornamentation?

When I speak of ornamentation in traditional Irish instrumental music, I am referring to ways of altering or embellishing pieces of a melody that are between one and three eighth-note beats long. These alterations and embellishments are created mainly through the use of special fingered articulations (cuts and strikes) and inflections (slides), not through the addition of extra, ornamental notes.

The modern classical musician's view of ornamentation is quite different. *Ornamentation, A Question & Answer Manual*, a book written to help classical musicians understand ornamentation from the baroque era through the present, offers this definition: "Ornamentation is the practice of adding notes to a melody to allow music to be more expressive."[1]

Classical musicians who are newcomers to traditional Irish music naturally tend to bring this kind of thinking with them. However, as long as one overlays this "added note" model onto Irish ornamentation, it will be harder to gain fluency in the language of Irish music.

Too Much Borrowing from Classical Music

Most people who have attempted to codify traditional Irish flute and whistle playing have borrowed concepts and notation practices from classical music. This works fairly well in some areas and not well at all in others.

Ornamentation is one of the areas where such borrowing has not served us well. Over many years of teaching I have met a great number of players who are mystified by Irish ornamentation techniques. Most of them have not had personal access to good players. Struck by the beauty of what they hear but missing key knowledge, they often turn to books in their search for insight. I feel that most books published before *The Essential Guide to Irish Flute and Tin Whistle* borrowed too much from the language and notation of classical music in an attempt to define and describe traditional Irish ornamentation. While some of these efforts at explanation are helpful, many of them create and perpetuate misunderstandings.

Grace Notes vs. Articulations

Most of the confusion has arisen from the liberal and often vague employment of the *grace note*, as a term, a concept and a notation practice. I feel that this has severely limited our thinking, and that such use of grace notes is the chief cause of misunderstandings about Irish ornamentation.

Using the concept of the *articulation,* instead of the grace note, allows us to understand ornamentation much more clearly. For our purposes, I define an articulation as *the extremely brief sound that defines the beginning or attack of a note*. To articulate a note is to create or define its first moment of sound.

Two Ways to Articulate a Note

With the flute, we can articulate a note in two ways. One is to briefly stop and restart the flow of air that we direct into the flute. We do this with our tongue or glottis and call it *tonguing* or *throating*. (The latter is my term for using articulations formed in the throat.) When we restart the flow of air, we give the sound an attack by an action of our tongue or glottis. We perceive this attack as the beginning, or articulation, of a new note. We can call these *breath articulations*.

A very different way to articulate a note is through the use of a finger movement.

---

[1] Valery Lloyd and Carole L. Bigler, *Ornamentation, A Question & Answer Manual* (Van Nuys, California: Alfred Publishing Co., 1995), p. 8.

Imagine these two scenarios:

- You are playing a low G on your flute. Without interrupting the flow of air *in any way*, you lift the middle finger of your top hand (the hand nearest the embouchure hole of the flute) completely off its hole, and, as quickly as possible, you put it back down onto its hole. The air has continued to flow through the flute without interruption.

- You are playing a low G on your flute. Without interrupting the flow of air *in any way*, you throw the index finger of your bottom hand (the hand nearest the foot of the flute) at its finger hole, allowing the finger to *bounce* back as quickly as possible. Again, the air has continued to flow through the flute without interruption. (In its very brief moment of contact with the flute, your index finger closed the finger hole entirely.)

The first scenario yields a *fingered articulation* called a **cut**. By lifting and replacing the middle finger of your top hand, you are, technically speaking, creating an additional note. But if that note is brief enough we cannot discern its pitch or duration. We perceive it not as a *note*, but, instead, as the articulation of the G note that follows it. *It is critically important to understand this phenomenon of perception.*

The second scenario yields a fingered articulation called a **strike** (also known as a *tip*, *tap*, *slap*, or *pat*). By bouncing the index finger of your bottom hand off of its finger hole, you are, technically speaking, creating an additional note. But if that note is brief enough, we will not discern its pitch or duration. As with the cut, we perceive it not as a note but as the articulation of the G note that follows it.

If you are having trouble following this, please be patient. It will become clear in time. The focus and scope of this book does not allow me to elaborate at length on these matters, but I devote a great deal of time and attention to them in *The Essential Guide to Irish Flute and Tin Whistle* and *The Essential Tin Whistle Toolbox*.

Rooted in Bagpipe Traditions

Tin whistle and Irish flute ornamentation has its origin in the tradition of the *uilleann pipes*, the current bellows-blown bagpipe of Ireland, whose techniques in turn developed from those of the older *pastoral bagpipe* and *píob mór* (Great Irish Warpipes) traditions. The capabilities and limitations of these two antecedent bagpipes shed important light upon why many uilleann pipe, Irish flute and tin whistle ornamentation techniques have evolved as they have.

While playing a tune on one of these older forms of bagpipes, there was no way to stop and restart the flow of air (i.e., there was nothing analogous to tonguing or throating). Therefore, when playing two notes of the same pitch in succession, these pipers had to use a fingered articulation to establish the beginning of such a repeated note. These fingered articulations have come down to us as the cut and the strike. They in turn give rise to the multi-note ornaments that make use of cuts and strikes, namely *rolls* and *cranns*. (Very similar finger articulation techniques have evolved within other bagpipe traditions around the world.)

Bear in mind that cuts and strikes are not used only on repeated notes. They are often used when ascending or descending to a note (though strikes are not possible when ascending to some notes). For much more on this, see *The Essential Guide to Irish Flute and Tin Whistle* or *The Essential Tin Whistle Toolbox*.

Say Goodbye to Grace Notes

In most other books, the cut and strike have been presented and notated as *grace notes*, and this is where so much confusion arises.

Figure 3. A conventional, misleading way of notating a cut as a grace note.

Cuts and strikes are plentiful in Irish music. If you think of each cut and strike as an additional note unto itself (represented as a grace note), your thought-picture of the music will become very cluttered and rhythmically problematic.

Cuts and strikes are articulations that function in ways similar to breath articulations. But I know of no one who has suggested notating tongue or glottal articulations as grace notes. Breath articulations have no discernible duration. The same is true of well-played cuts and strikes.

A grace note, on the other hand, takes up a small but discernible amount of time, which has to be "stolen" either from the note preceding it or the note following. It also has a pitch that is meant to be identifiable, normally one of the notes of the scale in use at the time.

Neither of these properties of the grace note, i.e., discernible duration and identifiable pitch, apply to the *perceived* sounds of the cut and strike. And perception is what counts here, not scientifically measurable durations or pitches that are too brief for us to identify by ear. We hear well-played cuts and strikes as having *no* duration, as falling exactly on a beat, not before or after. They do not have an identifiable pitch, though we can perceive them as being either higher in pitch (the cut) or lower in pitch (the strike) than the notes they articulate (their parent notes).

Cuts and strikes cannot exist without their parent notes. You cannot play just a cut or just a strike, because they are not notes. They are merely the articulations of their parent notes.

When cuts and strikes are played well (and this takes practice), we don't hear music crowded and cluttered by tiny grace notes that are somehow squeezed in between the main notes of the tune. Instead, we hear rhythmic clarity. We simply hear the notes of the tune articulated in a subtle variety of ways. Some are smoothly connected to the previous note. Some are tongued or throated. Some are smoothly connected to the previous note *and* articulated with a cut. Some are tongued and cut at the same time. And so on.

A Cut Notation

Since a cut is an articulation, I notate it as a slash placed over its parent note.

Figure 4. A note that is articulated with a cut.

This is a simple, clean notation that reflects the reality of the cut's sound and function. There is only one note here, not two. There is no indication or implication of pitch or duration for the cut. The application of this symbol is similar to that of other commonly used symbols, such as staccato markings or accents, which are placed above the notes they affect.

Fingering Notation

In this book I call the hand closest to the embouchure hole of the flute the **top hand**. The hand nearest the other end, the foot of the flute, I call the **bottom hand**. Either of these can be the right or left hand, though most people play with the left hand as the top hand and the right hand as the bottom hand. It seems to be in our nature to prefer using our dominant hand as the bottom hand.

I call the top hand index finger T1, the top hand middle finger T2, and the top hand ring finger T3. Similarly, I call the bottom hand index finger B1, the bottom hand middle finger B2, and the bottom hand ring finger B3. These labels works equally well for right-handed and left-handed players. See Figure 5 on the next page.

In addition to left-handedness, there may be other reasons why a person might choose to play the flute left-handed, for example due to a hand injury or other physical limitation. Or a player may have first learned to play the tin whistle before moving on to the flute, using her right hand as the top hand. (There is no intrinsic advantage to using either the right or left-handed hold on the tin whistle.) Bear in mind, however, that the flute's embouchure hole is almost always made to be blown into from the right-handed side, and keyed flutes are made to be played right-handed as matter of course. One can order a custom-made left-handed flute, but almost all the flutes already on the market are designed to be played right-handed.

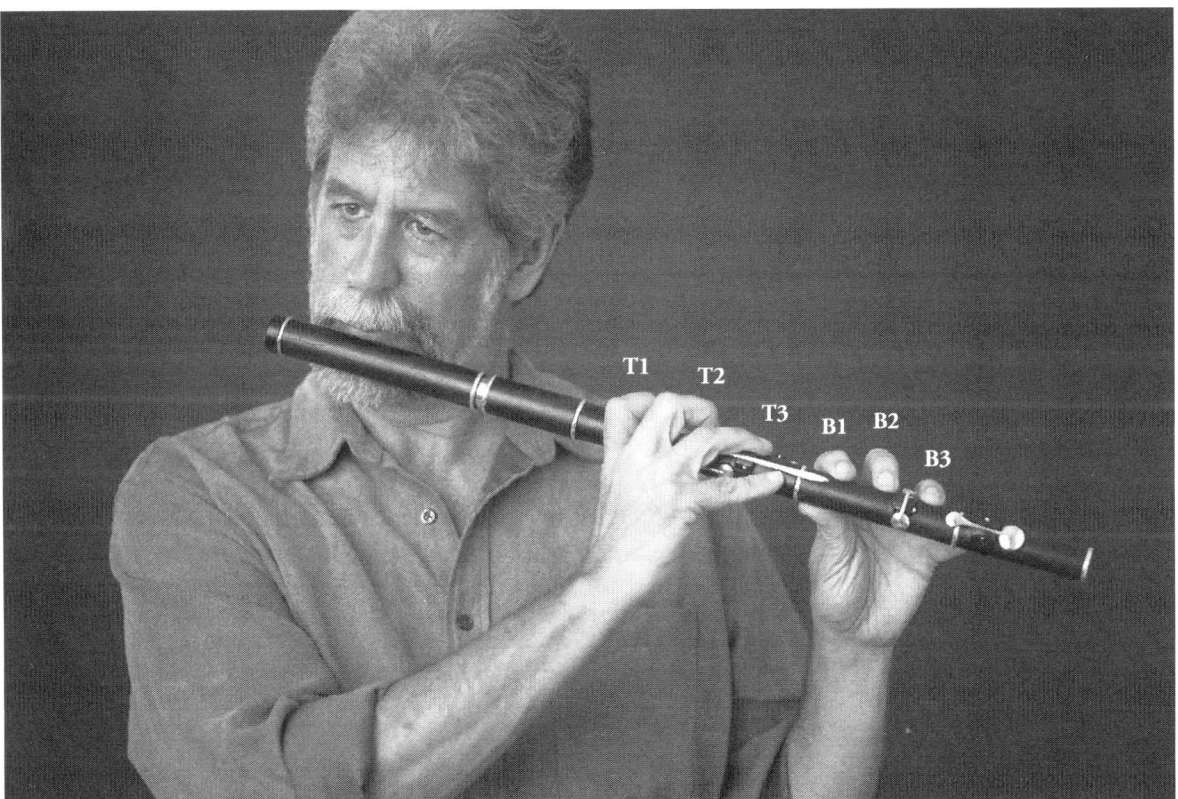

Figure 5. The right-handed hold (upper photo) and the left-handed hold (lower photo), with fingering indications.

THE MOVEMENT AND FINGERING OF THE CUT

The movement of the cut is a very small and quick lift of a finger completely off its hole and the immediate replacement of that finger. When executed well it may be almost invisible to an observer. The finger barely needs to move from the hole, although it does need to completely uncover it.

In my opinion, a cut should almost always sound as well-defined and crisp as possible. Using the optimum fingerings is a great help in achieving this. To this end, I use fingerings that are somewhat different from those used by most players.

In my method, for each of the notes D, E, F♯, G and A, in both low and high registers, the lowest covered hole remains covered (i.e., the covered hole that is furthest from the embouchure hole). I perform the cut by quickly uncovering and re-covering the next hole up (toward the embouchure hole). Therefore D is cut with B2, E with B1, F♯ with T3, G with T2, and A with T1.

The exception to this procedure occurs when cutting B. You cut B with T1, as this is the only finger available for the job.

It is very important to keep your hands relaxed when learning and using cuts. Though it seems to be human nature to do so, be sure you don't tense up while trying to make your cuts quick and crisp.

For more on cut fingering choices, see *The Essential Guide to Irish Flute and Tin Whistle* or *The Essential Tin Whistle Toolbox.*

WHY DO WE CALL CUTS AND STRIKES ORNAMENTS?

Cuts and strikes, our fingered articulations, are commonly referred to by Irish musicians as "ornaments." Since this is such a long-established custom, I feel I must conform to it. Well-played cuts and strikes do have a fleeting pitch element. Perhaps for that reason they convey an "ornamental quality" to our ear. Other articulations that do not have a pitch element, such as tonguing and throating, do not seem to strike us as ornamental.

Still, I feel it is best to think of cuts and strikes as articulations. Since they are so central to Irish flute ornamentation, the ramifications of conceiving of them this way are quite far-reaching.

MID-NOTE CUTS

Sometimes you will want to place a cut in the midst of a note instead of at its start (in effect dividing the note into two). I call this kind of cut a **mid-note cut**. In Irish tunes that have a regular pulse, it usually sounds best to place the mid-note cut squarely on a subdivision of that pulse.

Here is an example of a mid-note cut placed halfway through a quarter note:

Figure 6. The first measure of the reel The Cameronian, *showing a mid-note cut.*
***CD #2, track 57.** You will find the complete tune on p. 63.*

In Figure 6, above, note that the cut symbol is not placed directly above the quarter note, but to its right, halfway between it and the next note. This is meant to show that the cut occurs at a point exactly halfway through the duration of the quarter note. This would sound the same as what is shown below in Figure 7.

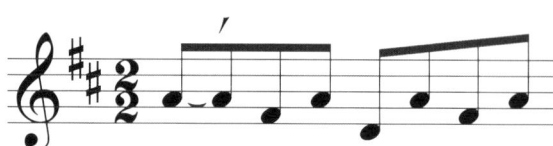

Figure 7. The same measure from The Cameronian, *notated a bit differently. Here the measure begins with two tied eighth notes instead of a quarter note. The cut articulates the second of these eighth notes.*

THE PHYSICAL MOVEMENTS AND FINGERINGS OF THE STRIKE

The strike is well named, for its crisp sound results from its percussive nature. In performing a strike you "throw" your finger at its tone hole so that it hits the instrument at a high velocity. Due to that velocity, the finger bounces back of its own accord, making it unnecessary to lift the finger off its hole. As with the cut, your fingers must be relaxed, though not limp, when performing a strike.

Unlike cut fingerings, strike fingerings seem to be universally agreed upon. As a rule, and this one has no exceptions, a strike on any given note is performed on the open tone hole closest to the embouchure hole. On the note E a strike is performed with B3. For F♯ you strike with B2, for G with B1, for A with T3, for B with T2, for C♯ with T1, and for C♯ also with T1. On Irish flute you cannot do a strike on D, and strikes are not often used on C♮ and C♯.

A Strike Notation

Since a strike is an articulation, I notate it by placing a V over its parent note.

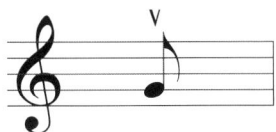

Figure 8. A note that is articulated with a strike.

This symbol graphically illustrates the downward velocity, impact and rebound of the strike. It is a simple, clean notation that reflects the reality of the strike's sound and function. Neither pitch nor duration are indicated or implied. There is only one note here, not two. Just like the cut, and for the same reasons, the strike is not a grace note. (Please don't confuse this symbol with the up-bow indication for bowed string instruments.)

Multi-Note Ornaments

Most **multi-note ornaments** are constructed by combining, in sequence, two, three or four articulated notes of eighth, sixteenth or, rarely, thirty-second-note durations. These notes are almost always slurred[2] together. The number of possible combinations is enormous, but only a fairly small number of them are used in Irish music.

In order to ensure that this tune collection is accessible to a wide range of players, I use only three of the multi-note ornaments in the transcriptions and recordings: long rolls, short rolls and long cranns. Although I do not use short cranns in this collection, I will describe them on p. 22. You may learn about all of the multi-note ornaments, including the widely-used condensed forms of rolls, in *The Essential Guide to Irish Flute and Tin Whistle*.

Long and Short Forms of Rolls and Cranns

Rolls and cranns exist in **long form** (three eighth-note beats in duration) and **short form** (two eighth-note beats in duration). The classification of rolls as long and short is widely recognized by traditional players. The classification of cranns as long and short seems to be less widespread.

Normal View and Exploded View

In the following pages you will encounter notated musical examples that are given in normal view, exploded view, or both. (For an example, see Figure 10 on the next page.)

Exploded view shows what happens inside of each multi-note ornament. Each of the ornament's constituent notes are depicted, along with each note's articulation (cut, strike; tongued/throated or slurred).

Normal view represents the multi-note ornament as either a quarter note or a dotted quarter note with a special symbol above it. This is how I represent such ornaments in the tune transcriptions.

---

[2] Here I am using the word "slur" to mean the connecting of a group of two or more notes such that only the first note of the group has a breath articulation. Thus a slurred group of notes is played using an uninterrupted, continuous stream of air. Any note in the slurred group may have a fingered articulation (cut or strike).

THE LONG ROLL

The **long roll** is the most commonly used multi-note ornament. It is something very simple and lovely: *a group of three slurred eighth notes of the same pitch, each one having a different articulation.*

- The first note is either tongued, throated, or slurred into from the preceding melody note.
- The second note is cut.
- The third note is struck.

What I have just described looks like this:

*Figure 9. A long roll on G, shown in exploded view. CD #2, **track 58**.*

USING AN ACCEPTED SYMBOL FOR THE LONG ROLL

There is already a symbol in common usage for rolls. Pat Mitchell, in his book *The Dance Music of Willie Clancy*,[3] writes that Breandán Breathnach, in his influential series of tune collections *Ceol Rince na hÉireann*,[4] devised this symbol to stand for all types of rolls and cranns.

Unlike Breathnach, I use this symbol very specifically, as shown below in Figure 10, to indicate the long roll only. I give other types of rolls and cranns different symbols, as you will soon see.

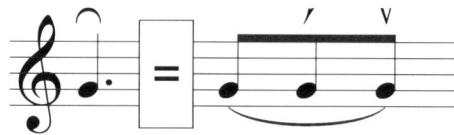

Figure 10. The symbol for a long roll on G, shown in normal view and exploded view.

Note that this crescent shaped symbol is placed above a dotted quarter note. The long roll is three eighth-note beats in duration, the same total duration as a dotted quarter note.

In some of the tune transcriptions you will see the long roll symbol placed above an eighth note or quarter note. For more on such situations, see "Rolls in Hornpipes" on p. 25 and "An Unusual Long Roll Notation" on p. 26.

CLEARING AWAY SOME FOG

Before the publication of *The Essential Guide to Irish Flute and Tin Whistle*, the long roll was almost always described and taught as a five-note ornament, due to the prevailing custom of thinking of cuts and strikes as grace notes. Add two grace notes to the three principal notes of the roll and you have five notes. Here's the problem with the five-note concept: when you listen to a well-played long roll, *you only hear three notes.*

Remember that cuts and strikes are not to be thought of as notes. We should think of them as articulations. Once that is understood, it follows that the notion of the five-note long roll represents an unnecessary and misleading complication. (The long roll is *not* a "turn," an ornament used in classical music traditions.)

---

[3] Pat Mitchell, *The Dance Music of Willie Clancy*, 2nd ed. (Dublin: Mercier Press, 1977), p. 12.
[4] Breandán Breathnach, *Ceol Rince na hÉireann*, Vol. 1 (Dublin: An Gúm, 1963).

Ill-Conceived Notation

Figure 11 shows some examples of misleading five-note long roll notation, taken from published whistle and flute tutors.

Figure 11. Examples of misleading five-note long roll notation.

None of these examples depict what a well-played long roll sounds like. None accurately convey its rhythm. All imply that the pitch of the cut and strike are identifiable and significant. None of them show that the sounds of the cut and the strike are qualitatively different from each other.

If anyone unfamiliar with the sound of a well-played long roll tried to accurately reproduce what was notated in these examples, they would not be playing a long roll.

When one is first learning cuts and strikes and cannot yet make them brief enough, a long roll will indeed sound as if it has five notes. Perhaps since everyone started out playing them that way we have retained some vestige of our old perceptions in our notation practices.

But why not notate them the way they sound when played *well*, especially since such a notation is much simpler to read and write?

The Short Roll

The **short roll** can be most easily grasped as a long roll without its first eighth note. Thus the short roll is *a group of two slurred eighth notes of the same pitch, each one having a different articulation*. The first note is cut, and the second is struck. What I have just described looks like this:

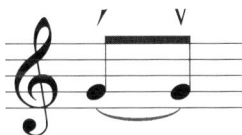

Figure 12. A short roll on G, shown in exploded view. **CD #2, track 59.**

It is essential to understand that the short roll occupies a total of only *two* eighth-note beats, whereas the long roll occupies three.

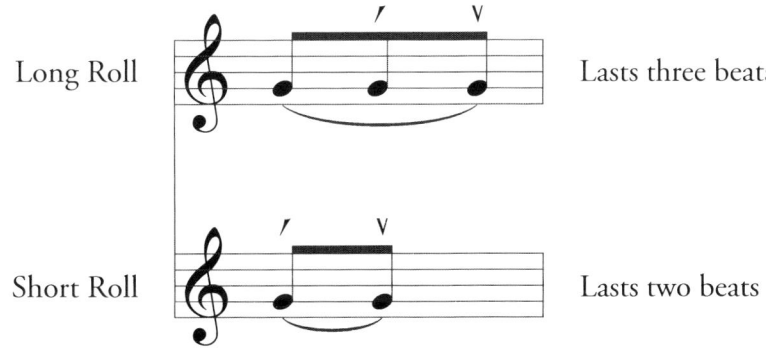

Figure 13. A comparison of long and short rolls.

A Short Roll Symbol

I have modified the symbol commonly used for rolls to create a symbol specifically for the short roll.

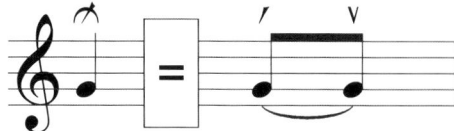

Figure 14. A short roll on G, shown in normal view and exploded view.

Note well that the short roll symbol appears above a quarter note. The short roll is only two eighth-note beats in duration, i.e., the same duration, in total, as a quarter note.

Notice that the short roll symbol is the long roll symbol with a slash through it. This shows that the short roll is a shortened form of the long roll. The slash, the symbol for the cut, also draws attention to the fact that a cut initiates the short roll.

Now That the Fog Has Cleared

By now you are thoroughly familiar with my opinion that cuts and strikes are articulations, not grace notes or notes of any kind. Thus you understand that the short roll is a two-note ornament, and not a four-note ornament as it has been described in most whistle and flute tutors published prior to *The Essential Guide to Irish Flute and Tin Whistle*. Figure 15, below, shows some examples of four-note short roll notation taken from these whistle and flute tutors.

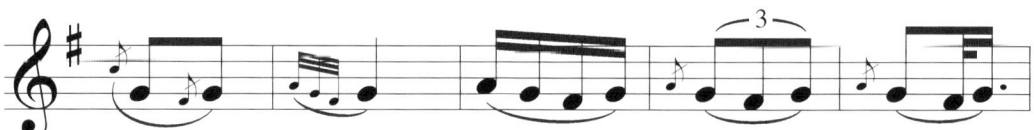

Figure 15. Examples of misleading four-note short roll notation.

These examples are incorrect and misleading. None of them look like what a short roll sounds like. None accurately convey the rhythm of the short roll. They all imply that the pitch of the cut and strike are identifiable and significant. None of them show that the sounds of the cut and the strike are qualitatively different from each other. If anyone unfamiliar with the sound of a well-played short roll tried to reproduce what is notated in these examples, they would not be playing a short roll.

It's best when notation represents the actual sound, especially when that notation is much simpler to read and write.

The Rhythms of Long and Short Rolls

When learning to play long and short rolls it is critically important to learn to play them with an absolutely dead-even rhythm. Each eighth note should be articulated right on its beat. You will not want to play rolls this evenly in every situation, but you will need to be able to do so when playing tunes at very fast tempos. The evenly-played roll is a solid base from which you can depart and experiment.

Short rolls almost always begin on a pulse or strong beat. Not so with long rolls. It is very important to know how each long roll relates to the underlying pulse of the music. When the first eighth note of a long roll does *not* fall on a pulse or strong beat, either the second or third eighth note always does. You want to be sure to place on-pulse notes accurately on their beats. For an in-depth discussion of why this is so, see *The Essential Guide to Irish Flute and Tin Whistle*.

Long Cranns

It is not possible to play a roll on D on an Irish flute because there is no way to strike a D. Yet D is such a critically important note in this music. How can we use ornamentation to draw attention to it?

One answer is the **crann**. The crann is an ornament that probably originated in the uilleann piping tradition. It makes use only of cuts.

Cranns are traditionally played not only on D but sometimes on E as well, especially by pipers. They can be played on other notes, too, but we rarely hear that with traditional flute and whistle players, who seem to prefer rolls over cranns where rolls are possible.

The **long crann** is composed of four slurred notes: an eighth note, two sixteenth notes, plus another eighth note. The second, third and fourth notes are cut.

Figure 16. A long crann on D, shown in exploded view. **CD #2, track 60.**

A Long Crann Symbol

I indicate a long crann as shown below.

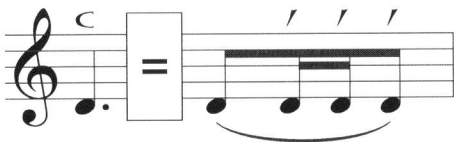

Figure 17. A long crann on D, shown in normal view and exploded view.

You can think of the crann symbol as the letter C (for crann), or as the long roll symbol turned on its side. Note well that the symbol appears above a dotted quarter note. The long crann is three eighth-note beats in duration, the same total duration as a dotted quarter note.

Fingering the Three Consecutive Cuts in Cranns

The consecutive cuts in cranns are not performed with just one finger.

Uilleann pipers often perform these cuts with three different fingers. Many flute and whistle players have directly adopted such piping fingerings to their instruments. Cutting D with a finger as far upstream (i.e., toward the embouchure) as T3 works very well on the pipes. But the responsiveness of this fingering on the flute is not as good, and it can be particularly weak in the high register. (The sluggishness of this response varies from one flute to another.)

I find that both long and short cranns sound tighter and more well-defined on the flute if you finger their cuts as follows: Play the first cut with B2, the normal cut fingering for D. Play the second cut with the next finger upstream, i.e., B1. For the third cut, go back to using the normal D cut fingering, B2. To see how this works on a low D long crann, see Figure 18, below.

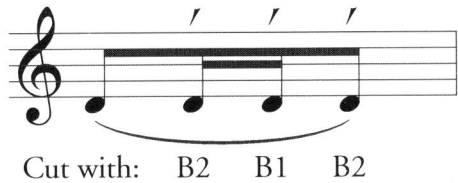

Figure 18. Recommended fingerings for the cuts in a long crann on D.

This fingering pattern allows you to change fingers for each cut of the crann and still use the most responsive cuts possible. Beginning and ending with B2 enables you to use the most responsive cut fingering twice, for the two cuts that fall on the most important subdivisions of the beat. I recommend fingering cranns this way on all sizes of whistles and flutes.

The Short Crann

The **short crann** is composed of three notes: two sixteenth notes plus an eighth note. All three notes are cut. Note that when you remove the first note of a long crann (an eighth note), what remains is a short crann.

Figure 19. A short crann on D, shown in exploded view. **CD #2, track 60** *(heard after Figure 16).*

The short crann is quite tricky to play in context (as is the short roll) because it is usually not preceded by a note of the same pitch. The long crann on the other hand, like the long roll, starts with an uncut note of the same pitch as that of the first cut note. This makes its first cut the easiest kind, the cut on a repeated note.

Sometimes you will hear players leave out the first cut of the short crann. This results in a simpler, softer crann with less attack. I encourage you to learn to play the short crann with all three cuts. You may then choose to omit the first cut as a matter of musical expression, not of technical limitation. You will find that it is sometimes easier to execute the full three-cut short crann when you also articulate its first note by tonguing or throating.

A Short Crann Symbol

I notate a short crann as shown below.

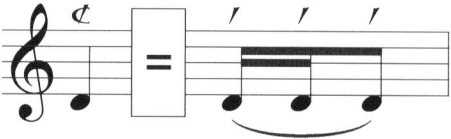

Figure 20. A short crann on low D, shown in normal view and exploded view.

The short crann symbol is that of the long crann with a slash through it. This shows that the short crann is a shortened or truncated form of the long crann. The slash, being the symbol for the cut, also draws attention to the fact that a cut note initiates the short crann.

Note well that the symbol appears above a quarter note. The short crann is only two eighth-note beats in duration, the same total duration as a quarter note.

Alternatives to the Crann

The crann is a difficult ornament to master. Many traditional players make use of small melodic variations in place of cranns.

Figure 21 shows the long crann while Figure 22 shows one of the most commonly played alternatives to it.

Figure 21. A long crann on low D.

Figure 22. A melodic alternative to a long crann on low D. **CD #2, track 61.**

A similar variant can be used in place of a short crann.

Figure 23. A short crann on low D.

Figure 24. A melodic alternative to a short crann on low D. **CD #2, track 62.**

This same variant can be used, played an octave higher, to take the place of a short crann on high D. Or, you could use this one:

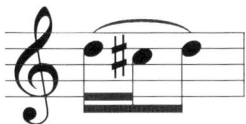

Figure 25. A melodic alternative to a short crann on high D. **CD #2, track 62** *(heard after Figure 24).*

As a fingering convenience, you may leave B1, B2 and B3 on their holes when fingering the quick C♯ shown above. Since it is preceded and followed by a D, this makes for better economy of motion.

The Slide

In several ways, the **slide** is quite different from the cut and strike. First, it is not an articulation. It is an inflection. It is not played or heard as an instantaneous event like the cut or the strike. It is a continuous, moving alteration of a note's pitch. In the classical world, the slide is sometimes referred to as a *portamento*.

Some Irish players refer to a slide as a "slur" or "smear," but "slur" has another, more widely accepted meaning. (See the footnote on page 17.) It is therefore best not to use the word "slur" for a slide.

When I speak of a slide I am referring to a musical gesture that is accomplished using a finger technique. Note that pitch slides can also be accomplished by breath techniques, quite independent of the fingers. Fingered slides, however, offer more in speed and agility.

The cut and strike create the attacks of their parent notes and are therefore fixed in their temporal relationships to them. The slide exists independent of these considerations. The concept of a parent note is not always useful in regard to the slide. A slide can begin before the attack of a note, or after. It can be very brief or very long. It can be a way to move from one note to another and can therefore affect both notes. The slide is the free spirit of single-note ornaments. You can get carried away with it if you don't watch out, giving your playing a slurpy, even a drunken feeling.

Slides can rise or fall in pitch, but rising slides are used more often than falling slides.

The Physical Movement of the Slide

When you slide, you are gradually, and sometimes only partially, covering or uncovering a finger hole in such a way that the pitch of the note you are playing at that moment glides up or down to the desired destination. By the way, the word "slide" refers to what happens to the *pitch* of the affected note or notes, not necessarily what the finger does to achieve that sound. Sometimes you do slide the finger, but other times you may tilt, rock, or roll it slightly instead.

Sometimes the destination of a slide is an alternate fingering. For instance, when sliding from B up to C, you move T1 slightly off of its hole until you reach a half-hole[5] fingering for C.

Sliding is easy and natural on the Irish flute, tin whistle, and uilleann pipes since the fingers come into direct contact with the finger holes. Sliding is possible, but not as natural, on the Boehm-system flute because of the key mechanisms that intervene between the fingers and the tone holes themselves. The natural ease of sliding with the simple-system instruments is certainly one of the reasons why the Irish flute is preferred over modern flutes by almost all players. (Another is the greater ease and flexibility in employing finger vibrato on simple-system instruments.)

The finger movement of the slide should be one that leaves your hand in good playing position once the slide is complete. You'll find much more on this and other aspects of slides in both *The Essential Guide to Irish Flute and Tin Whistle* and *The Essential Tin Whistle Toolbox*.

Two Classes of Slides

Slides fall into two classes according to:

- their relationship to the melody, and
- the fingerings they require

The **simple slide** directly connects two consecutive notes in a melody, "filling in" the interval between them. Usually this kind of slide moves in the same direction as the melody. In sliding from one melody note to the next, the only finger or fingers moving are the same ones that, in normal playing, you would use to move directly (i.e., without sliding) from the first note to the second. For example, when moving from A up to B using a simple slide, one simply removes T2 gradually from its hole.

The **added-finger slide** requires the involvement of an additional finger, one that is not normally used in moving from the first melody note to the next. In most cases, the pitch slide does not occur within the interval formed by the two melody notes in question, but outside of this interval, and it moves in the direction opposite to that of the melodic movement. For example, when moving from G down to E and using an added-finger slide to inflect the E, you put down B1 and B2 in normal fashion to move from G to E, and, at the same time, B3 covers all or part of its hole and immediately moves smoothly off of it to produce a pitch slide up to E from below. The melodic movement from G to E is downward, but the movement of the pitch slide is upward, rising to E from below.

Both simple and added-finger slides can occur in rising and falling forms.

It's important to note that the faster you perform a slide, the more subtle is its effect. On the whole, I much prefer subtle slides. Most of the slides you encounter in this book's tune transcriptions are meant to be fast, subtle ones.

Sliding Up to C

The half-hole fingering for C♮ is used more by whistle players than it is by flute players, especially when a tune moves directly from B up to C. I believe this is the case because inexpensive, mass-produced whistles (which were the only ones one could purchase in older times) often lack a suitable, in-tune cross-fingering for C♮.

For an example of this special use of sliding, see tune 29, *Fraher's Jig*, on p. 58 (B-part, m. 3).

---

[5] "Half-holing" refers to the practice of only partially covering a tone hole in order to play a pitch that falls in between the pitches produced by fully covering the tone hole in question and fully opening that tone hole.

A Slide Notation

Figures 26 and 27 show symbols for rising and falling slides.

Figures 26 and 27. A rising slide and a falling slide. **CD #2, track 63.**

Rolls in Hornpipes

Irish dance music is rarely, if ever, played in an absolutely even rhythmic fashion, i.e., with all eighth notes identical in duration and weight. The unevenness, or lilt, in reels, jigs and other types of tunes can be quite subtle and often goes unnoticed.

However, hornpipes, mazurkas, schottisches, germans, flings, barn dances and some set dances are normally played with an overt, intentional unevenness of rhythm that is not as subtle. In what follows I will speak only of hornpipes, but the information given also applies to those other tune types, for example tune 92, *The Blackbird* (set dance, p. 79), tune 122, *An Cúisín Bán* (set dance, p. 95), and tune 149, *John Doherty's Mazurka* (p. 110).

I notate hornpipes as if they were played with an even eighth-note subdivision of the pulse – in the same manner that reels are notated – but with occasional eighth-note triplets. However, hornpipes are usually not played as evenly as is implied by this notational style. Instead, they are usually played unevenly, with an overt lilt.

It follows, then, that when playing rolls (long and short) in hornpipes, you play them within the prevailing unevenness or lilt you are employing at the time. For a detailed treatment of this subject, see Chapter 14, "Rolls in Tunes with Overtly Uneven Subdivisions of the Beat," in *The Essential Guide to Irish Flute and Tin Whistle*.

Though I cannot go into much detail on this here, I would like to explain one unusual presentation of long rolls that comes up in some hornpipes and set dances, such as tune 74, the hornpipe *The Blackbird* (p. 73).

In the first and second ending of the A-part of *The Blackbird*, and in the second ending of the B-part, you will see a long roll symbol placed above a quarter note. (A quarter note has a total duration equal to only two eighth-note beats.) See Figure 28, below.

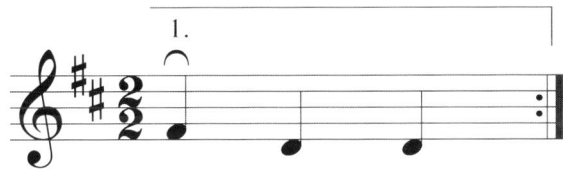

Figure 28. An unusual quarter-note long roll in tune 74, the hornpipe The Blackbird.
You will find the complete tune on p. 73.

Normally, long rolls occur over the course of three eighth-note beats, i.e., the total duration of a dotted quarter note (as shown in Figure 10 on p. 18).

In this case, however, the long roll is played using the rhythm of an eighth-note triplet. Each of the three notes of the roll are equal in duration, and their durations, when added together, equal the length of one (undotted) quarter note. Figure 29, below, shows this long roll in exploded view.

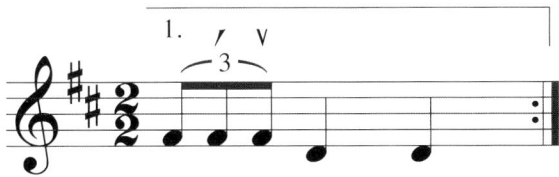

Figure 29. Exploded view of a quarter-note long roll in tune 74, The Blackbird. **CD #2, track 64.**

An Unusual Long Roll Notation

In some circumstances, the long roll symbol appears above a note that is not a dotted quarter note or a quarter note. An example of this occurs in tune 4, the jig *Breeches Mary*.

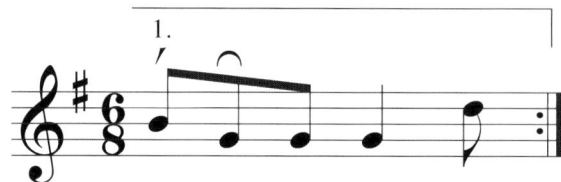

Figure 30. The first ending of the B-part of tune 4, Breeches Mary.
CD #2, track 65. *You will find the complete tune on p. 49.*

The long roll begins on the second eighth-note subdivision of the pulse, and ends with the note that falls on the following pulse, the quarter note G.

The roll is *not* condensed into the duration of a single eighth note, an impression one might get from this notation. In this collection I do not use condensed rolls, but rolls can be condensed and often are. For a thorough exploration of condensed rolls, see *The Essential Guide to Irish Flute and Tin Whistle*.

The following alternative notation would look awkward, even though it would be conventional in the sense that the long roll symbol, as is customary, appears above a dotted quarter note.

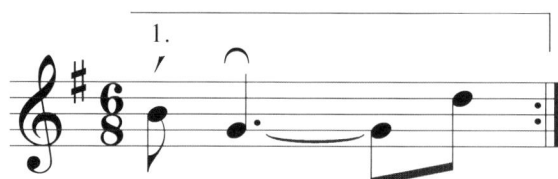

Figure 31. An awkward way of notating what is shown above in Figure 30.

Notating the music as shown in Figure 30 makes the most sense, especially since the long roll is optional. If one chooses not to play a long roll here, one would prefer to see the three Gs notated individually.

For examples of long rolls that begin on the third subdivision of the pulse, see the A-part of tune 7, the jig *Thirsty for Drink* (p. 50), the A-part and C-part of tune 15, the jig *Tell Her I Am, three-part version* (p. 53) and the B-part of tune 16, the jig *Tell Her I Am, two-part version* (p. 53).

Chapter Two: Modes and Other Notation Matters

In addition to ornamentation symbols, there are other notation practices used in the tune transcriptions which may be unfamiliar to some readers.

The Breath Mark

The breath mark – ' – is a symbol widely used in classical music to indicate when a wind player may take a breath. In that tradition, it is placed slightly above the top line of the staff and in between two notes, or above a rest. This conveys to the wind player that she may take a breath between the two notes, taking a bit of time away from the end of the first of those notes to do so, or simply that the rest provides a good place to breathe.

For the non-wind player, the breath mark indicates a place to create a brief space in the music.

My use of the breath mark is quite different. I explain this on pp. 36-37.

Repeat Signs

I use some common-practice repetition indications in the tune transcriptions. In case you are unfamiliar with them:

- "D.C." stands for *da capo,* an Italian phrase meaning "from the beginning," or literally "from the head." This tells you to repeat from the beginning of the tune.
- "D.S." stands for *dal segno,* an Italian phrase meaning "from the sign." This tells you to repeat not from the beginning, but from a different location marked by a *segno* (i.e., "sign"). The *segno* looks like this: 𝄋 .
- A thin-thick double barline preceded by two dots (:||) is a left-facing repeat sign. It tells you to go back to an earlier right-facing repeat sign (||:), or, if there is none, back to the beginning of the tune.

Notes That Fall Below the Range of the Standard Irish Flute

Many of the tunes in Sections Two and Three include notes that fall below the low D of the standard Irish flute. When flute players come across such notes, we usually transpose them up an octave. (Some Irish and modern flutes, however, can play as low as B and so can play a few more of these low notes than other flutes can.)

In this book I suggest ways to change the tune when encountering notes that are too low for the standard Irish flute in D (i.e., notes lower than low D). The original too-low note (or notes) are still represented though, shown as open diamond-shaped noteheads without stems. Here is an example:

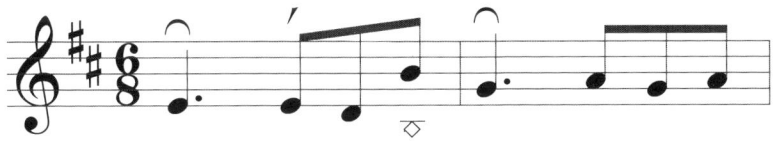

Figure 32. The first two measures of tune 95, The Orphan. *The tune has a B, shown here as an open diamond notehead, which is too low for the standard Irish flute. As shown in the normal notation, the player can play that note an octave higher.* **CD #2, track 66.** *You will find the complete tune on p. 84.*

Raising by an octave only the notes that *must* be raised can result in sudden leaps, up or down, by large intervals such as minor sevenths and major sixths. In some tunes this can be striking, intriguing and lovely, while in others it may feel jarring or arbitrary.

An alternative is to raise not only the notes that must be raised, but also other notes that come before and/or after. This incorporates the below-range note (or notes) into an entire phrase which is then elevated into a higher register. Such new phrases can lend cohesion and bring a fresh and surprising character to a tune.

When I demonstrate the approach I have just described, you'll see open diamond noteheads for notes that fall both below and *within* the range of the flute. An example appears on the next page.

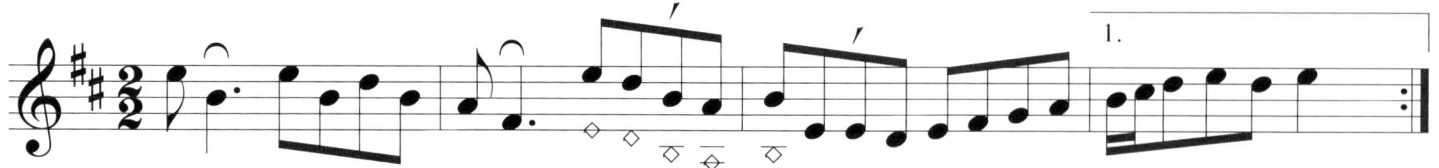

Figure 33. The last four measures of the A-part of tune 114, The Humours of Lissadell.
Five notes are transposed up an octave. The first two notes (E and D) are not too low for the flute, but the A and Bs are.
CD #2, track 67. *You will find the complete tune on p. 91.*

There are several examples of this approach to register shifting in tune 115, *The Green Hills of Tyrol*. (See p. 92 and CD #2, track 21.)

Since it is so easy to change the register of notes on the flute (most fingerings are the same in both octaves), one can transpose notes with spontaneity. Or you can take a more studied approach, as I did with *The Green Hills of Tyrol*.

You can, of course, also transpose high notes down into the low register at will.

I find that some tunes with register-shifted notes sound best when they are played along with an instrument that can play the notes in their original register. Others stand well even when a flute is the only melody instrument.

Mode Signatures Instead of Key Signatures

Throughout this book I use "mode signatures" instead of key signatures. The two look the same, but have somewhat different meanings. I hope the following information on modes will help make the distinction clear.

The Modal Nature of Irish Music

In today's common practice of western classical and popular music, almost all tonal music is considered to be in either a major or minor key, that is, based upon the central use of certain major or minor scales. The major and natural minor scales have early historical roots and are only two of seven modes that came to form the tonal basis for Gregorian chant and the rest of western medieval and renaissance music.

The word "mode" has a number of meanings, but in this case I use it to refer to "the selection of tones, arranged in a scale, which form the basic tonal substance of a composition."[1] There are many more than seven modes in world musical traditions, but for the moment we need only be concerned with the seven so-called "church modes" of western European music.

The vast majority of traditional Irish tunes make use of only four of these modes: the **Ionian** (which is commonly called the major scale), the **Dorian**, the **Mixolydian**, and the **Aeolian** (which is commonly called the natural minor scale).

Each of the seven modes contains a unique sequence of five whole steps (major seconds) and two half steps (minor seconds) that occur as you ascend through its scale.

In the following figures, the half steps are indicated by slurs.

One simple way to listen to and get to know these modes is to play ascending scales on Irish flute in D, using only the notes of its natural scale: D, E, F♯, G, A, B and C♯. Starting on low D and playing in this manner, you hear the notes and intervals of the D Ionian mode. Starting on E, you hear the E Dorian mode, and so on, as shown in Figure 34 on the next page. Note well the locations of the half steps in each mode.

---

[1] Willi Apel, p. 452.

Figure 34: The seven so-called church modes, as played using the natural scale of an Irish flute in D. **CD #2, *track 68.***

Another way to explore these modes is to play ascending scales on only the white keys of a keyboard instrument. Starting on C, you hear the notes and intervals of the C Ionian mode. Starting on D, you hear the D Dorian mode, and so on.

THE TONAL CENTER OF THE MODE

Each mode has a tonal center, which is the first and lowest note of its scale. In Irish music, this tonal center can reside on any one of various pitches, most commonly D, E, G, A or B. We often say, for example, that a tune in the Mixolydian mode with a tonal center of D is in "D Mixolydian." Similarly, a tune in the Dorian mode that has a tonal center of E is in "E Dorian." The tune will usually come to rest on the pitch of its tonal center at various points, especially at the ends of some of its important phrases.

Those who are familiar with major and minor scales (i.e., the Ionian and Aeolian modes) may find it helpful to understand the Dorian and Mixolydian modes in terms of how they differ from the Ionian and Aeolian.

- The Mixolydian mode is like the Ionian (major scale) with a flatted or lowered seventh note.
- The Dorian mode is like the Aeolian (natural minor scale) with a raised or sharped sixth note.

These comparisons are shown on the next page in Figure 35. You might try playing through them or singing them. Note how only the position of the second half step differs in each comparison.

Figure 35. Comparisons between the Ionian and Mixolydian modes, and the Aeolian and Dorian modes. **CD #2, track 69**.

The combinations of mode and tonal center most commonly found in the repertoires of flute players, tin whistle players and uilleann pipers are shown below in Figure 36. (Note well the mode signatures.)

Figure 36: The modal scales most commonly used by Irish flute, tin whistle and uilleann pipe players. **CD #2, track 70.**

WATCH FOR MODE SIGNATURES

Note that Figure 36 uses the appropriate mode signature for each scale, instead of using accidentals.

All the tunes in this book are notated using mode signatures. Therefore, when you see a signature of two sharps, for example, don't assume that the music is in D major (Ionian) or its relative minor (B Aeolian). It could just as easily be in A Mixolydian or E Dorian. (See staves #1, 4, 5 and 8 in Figure 36, above.) I favor the use of mode signatures as they result in fewer accidentals and also reflect the true modal nature of Irish music.

You may have noticed that there are no flats in the mode signatures shown in Figure 36. Modal scales which include flats, such as G Dorian and F Ionian, are encountered in tunes that are played most commonly on the fiddle, banjo, accordion and other non-wind instruments. (This is also true of the modal scales which have no sharps or flats: D Dorian, G Mixolydian and A Aeolian.)

Players of keyed flutes and pipes can also play in these "flatter" modes. Unfortunately, I find that relatively few of them do. I encourage you to play tunes in these modes if you have a keyed Irish flute or a modern flute. You'll find 13 of them in "Section Three: Tunes Requiring the Use of Keys."

A Limitation of the Keyless Irish Flute in D

There are four notes that the keyless Irish flute in D cannot easily produce: E♭, F♮, G♯, and B♭. One can play these notes by employing the partial covering of tone holes (half-holing[2]) or by using cross-fingerings[3], but these techniques are impractical in many situations, especially when playing at moderate and faster speeds.

Playing on Keyless Irish Flutes Made in Keys Other Than D

One can obtain keyless Irish flutes in keys other than D. Playing these can make it possible for flute players who do not have a keyed instrument to play in modes that are not practical on a keyless Irish flute in D.

For instance, one can play tunes that are in D Dorian (a scale which includes F♮) by fingering them *as if* they were in E Dorian while playing on an Irish flute that is in the key of C. The C flute is built to play a whole step lower than the normal D flute. Since you are fingering the tune as if it were in a scale that is one whole step higher than its actual scale of D Dorian, these two factors cancel each other out and the tune sounds in the correct scale (D Dorian).

Here's another example: you can use a flute built in the key of E to play tunes that are in A Ionian (a scale which includes G♯). You would finger such tunes as if they were in G Ionian. Since the flute is built to play a whole step higher than the normal D flute, and you are fingering the tune as if it were in a scale that is one whole step lower than its actual scale, these two factors cancel each other out and the tune sounds in the correct scale (A Ionian).

To explore this further, see "Appendix: Playing Tunes on Non-D Flutes" on pp. 112-123. You may also wish to take a look at "Section Three: Tunes for Non-D Whistles" in the collection *150 Gems of Irish Music for Tin Whistle*. The tunes presented there, and the instructions on how to play them on whistles in keys other than D, can be applied equally well to keyless Irish flutes in keys other than D.

Outside the Modal Boundaries

There are many Irish tunes that don't fit neatly into the profile of any of these modes. In one tune you may find both the major and minor forms of the third, sixth or seventh scale degrees. Then there are tunes that use only five or six notes.

Some tunes employ notes that fall in between the half steps. This happens in particular in the area of C♮ to C♯ and F♮ to F♯ on the flute, whistle, and uilleann pipes.

C♮ is an especially variable note on the uilleann pipes which, according to Breandán Breathnach, possesses "several colors ... which are exploited to the full by the skillful performer. It lies approximately halfway between B and D"[4] – in other words, approximately halfway between the equal tempered C♮ and C♯. In fact, at least half the time C♮ is played according to our modern intonation expectations, but often, especially in tunes with a tonal center of G or D, the sharper "piping C" is used by traditional flute and whistle players. The pitch of C♮ can change even while playing the note.

On the keyless Irish flute, you can finger C♮ by using a cross-fingering or by half-holing. On a keyed flute you might also have the option of using a C♮ key. You can also play this "piping C" by using special fingerings which are explained in *The Essential Guide to Irish Flute and Tin Whistle*. All of these fingering options produce Cs with differing tone and pitch colors, which relate quite directly to the tradition of uilleann piping.

---

[2] "Half-holing" refers to the practice of only partially covering a tone hole in order to play a pitch that falls in between the pitches produced by fully covering the tone hole in question and fully opening that tone hole.

[3] John Smith and Joe Wolfe, in the International Congress on Acoustics, Rome, Session 8.09, pp. 14-15, describe cross fingering in this way: "Opening successive tone holes in woodwind instruments shortens the standing wave in the bore. However, the standing wave propagates past the first open hole, so its frequency can be affected by closing other tone holes further downstream. This is called cross fingering, and in some instruments is used to produce the 'sharps and flats' missing from their natural scales."

[4] Breandán Breathnach, *Folk Music & Dances of Ireland* (Dublin: The Talbot Press, 1971), p. 14.

The Passing C: Natural or Sharp?

When playing C as a quick passing note between B and D, Irish flute and whistle players will often play the note as a C♯, even if C♯ is not in the mode of the tune. This may be in large part because playing B – C♯ – D makes for an easier fingering sequence. The C♯ often goes by quickly enough that its altered pitch does not seem apparent.

This use of C♯ is an element of personal style, and preferences vary among players. As you will see in the tune transcriptions, most of the time I prefer the C♯.

On the Boehm-system flute, fingering C♮ in such situations is no harder than fingering C♯ – in fact sometimes it is easier. Therefore, Boehm-system flute players may tend to overlook altering C in this way, since it has no particular fingering benefit for them. It's also interesting to note that while C♯ tends to be flat on the Irish flute, it tends to be slightly sharp on the Boehm-system flute. This is another reason why Boehm-system flute players may prefer playing the passing C as a C♮.

For examples of this use of C♯, see *Thirsty for Drink* (tune 7, p. 50), *The Windy Gap* (tune 52, p. 66) and *O'Callaghan's* (tune 73, p. 73).

Chapter Three: Breathing and Phrasing

The flute and tin whistle are the only instruments of traditional Irish music that are not suited to continuous playing. We must interrupt the flow of sound in order to breathe. One could regard this as a handicap, or instead take advantage of the opportunity it presents. Since we must create breathing spaces, why not use these spaces to define clear musical phrases? That's exactly what skilled Irish flute players do, either consciously or by instinct.

Of course, singers must create breathing spaces as well.

When we create a breathing space, we end one musical phrase and begin another. A breathing space is like a punctuation mark – a comma, a semicolon, a period.

Fine players of non-wind instruments use space in a similar way, even though they are not obliged to. They know how important it is to make their instruments "sing." Leaving space is a crucial part of producing a singing quality.

For much more on these topics, see *The Essential Guide to Irish Flute and Tin Whistle.*

Articulate and Inarticulate Breathing

Articulate breathing illuminates the phrasing and natural contours of a tune. **Inarticulate breathing** disrupts the music and draws attention to itself. When your breathing is articulate, listeners naturally attend to the phrasing of the music, often not noticing your breathing at all. The location of an articulate breath is governed by musical choice more than the necessity to get more oxygen.

A Breath Is a Silent Note

In slow airs and other slow tunes, one can often take a quick breath between consecutive notes without disrupting the flow of the music. But with dance tunes it almost never works to play all the notes "as written," grabbing very quick breaths in between them. When you attempt this, you end up cheating certain notes of their full duration. This well-intentioned but ineffective strategy rarely affords you enough time to get the air you need, and your energy suffers as a result. You will likely end up breathing inarticulately and too frequently, disrupting the music and drawing attention to your attempts at getting enough air, perhaps even disturbing the steadiness of the music's pulse.

As with the sounding of each note, the taking of a breath can be, in and of itself, a rhythmic event, with a specific and accurate duration.

Creating a Breathing Space

Flute and whistle players create a space for breathing by:

- entirely omitting an eighth note of the melody, or
- shortening a longer note by the increment of one eighth note

Think of breathing places as *silent eighth notes*, or eighth-note rests.

An exception can occur in polkas, in which we sometimes create breathing spaces by omitting sixteenth notes. For more on this, see "The Special Case of Polkas" on p. 41.

Making Spontaneous Choices

Breathing choices are best when they are fluid and changeable, not predetermined. Why? For two reasons.

1. Your air needs will continually vary, depending upon many factors and conditions of the moment: the speed of the tune, how loud you want to play, whether you are sitting or standing, how well rested or tired you are (which affects how deeply you breathe), whether or not you recently ate a large meal, how well focused your embouchure is on a given day, even the altitude of the locale. Your need for oxygen should determine when you will prepare to create a breathing place.

2. Spontaneity of breathing is a fundamental tool for creating variation in traditional Irish music. When your breathing choices become spontaneously variable, so does the phrasing of your music. This makes for a more vital experience, for the listener and for you.

Classical wind players often predetermine the breathing places in each piece of music they play. Classical composers who write for wind instruments typically incorporate rests into their music to provide breathing opportunities for the player. Omitting any of a composer's carefully chosen notes is generally discouraged.

With traditional Irish dance music, flute players *must* omit or shorten notes. There are no built-in accommodations for breathing. Each tune is shared by all the melodic instruments of the tradition (wind and non-wind), and each player adapts the music to her instrument in particular ways.

Some Notes Are Essential, Others Are Not

It is revealing to discover that not every note of a tune is indispensable. You can leave certain notes out without compromising the tune. In fact omitting such notes can create pleasing variations.

On the other hand, there are many notes that you must *not* omit, and you must learn to discern the difference.

I advise you to omit as few notes as possible when you take a breath, and make your breaths quick and deep.

So, How Can We Define a Tune?

There is no simple answer to this question, but a traditional Irish tune is certainly not an established, unchangeable and unbroken sequence of notes, as one might presume by looking in printed collections. It is something much more fluid and multidimensional, something large and living that music notation cannot contain. When you leave notes out, shorten notes, and change the melody in small ways that are appropriate within the language of the tradition, you are staying true to the tune and keeping it vital.

Breathe Before You Have To

To breathe articulately, you must first attend to the physical requirements of deep breathing and the efficient use of your air supply. I cover these subjects in depth in *The Essential Guide to Irish Flute and Tin Whistle* and *The Essential Tin Whistle Toolbox*.

You may have noticed that when you get close to running out of air, your energies (mental, physical, and musical) begin to suffer. Make sure you don't let your lungs get this empty. Breathe before you have to.

If you are not used to taking deep breaths, or if you are using your air inefficiently, you may not have noticed how your energy can be undermined by an inadequate supply of air. Perhaps you are almost always short of air, breathing when you have to instead of when you might choose to. When air becomes plentiful, you can play with strong, vibrant energy and breath support. You can breathe articulately, breathing for phrasing rather than from an urgent need for oxygen.

Embouchure Development

If you are fairly new to flute playing, or are adjusting to a new flute, you may not yet be able to use your air with high efficiency. In this stage of development, you will need to breathe relatively frequently. Once your embouchure becomes more focused and refined, you'll be able to play for a longer time between breaths. This will give you much more freedom in your phrasing choices.

Note Omission and Note Shortening Become Second Nature

Like so many other technical aspects of playing Irish music on the flute, note omission and note shortening will become second nature with enough practice and attention. As you establish a habit of always tuning in to your body, you will continually become more aware of your momentary air supply status. More and more, you will relegate this awareness to a subsurface level of your mind, which will keep track of your air while you are having fun playing music. When you are approaching low air supply, you will feel it in your body, and you will improvise a musical way to leave out or shorten a note, take a quick, deep breath, and continue on your merry way with a plentiful stock of air.

When you leave out an eighth note in order to breathe, you may choose to still hear that note in your mind's ear. You might even finger the note. These strategies might help if leaving out notes sometimes throws you off the tune or off the beat. However, I feel it's important to let go of these devices as you become more accustomed to creating breathing spaces.

Never Omit a Note That Falls on a Pulse

Omitting an on-pulse note is inconsistent with the language of traditional Irish music, and represents the epitome of inarticulate breathing. If you omit such a note, knowledgeable players, listeners, and dancers may feel that you are punching a gaping hole into the flow of the tune. If you choose to do so anyway, for dramatic effect, know that you are tinkering with one of the fundamental underpinnings of the music and that some people will hear this as an indication of inexperience.

Well, Almost Never ...

There are two minor exceptions to the rule just given. They are discussed under "Breathing Strategy #1: Shortening a Long Note" on p. 38 and "Breathing in Slow-Moving Tunes" on p. 42.

So, Where Is the Pulse?

In reels, jigs, slides, hornpipes, polkas, schottisches, flings, barn dances, germans, strathspeys and marches there is a pattern of two strong recurring rhythmic pulses per measure, which is counted "**one**, two; **one**, two"; etc. These types of tunes are in **duple meter**. Most people tap their feet to these pulses, and "one" usually gets a bit more stress than "two."

In slip jigs, hop jigs, mazurkas and waltzes, there is a pattern of three strong recurring pulses per measure, which is counted "**one**, two, three; **one**, two, three"; and so on, with "one" getting a bit more stress than "two" or "three." These types of tunes are in **triple meter**.

In each tune type, the pulse is subdivided into smaller units of time. In reels, each pulse is subdivided into four equal parts, usually notated as eighth notes, and in jigs, each pulse is subdivided into three eighth-note parts. In the terminology of music theory, reels are in a **simple duple meter** and jigs are in a **compound duple meter**.

In reels, then, there are eight eighth-note beats per measure. The pulse we have been talking about falls on the first and fifth of these eighth-note beats. But the third and seventh beats carry some special weight too, though not as much as the first and fifth. Thus, there are two pulses existing concurrently in reels, the **primary pulse**, on one and five, and a **secondary pulse**, on three and seven.

In jigs, the pulse falls on the first and fourth eighth-note beats and there is no secondary pulse. To keep things relatively simple we will look only at reels and jigs here.

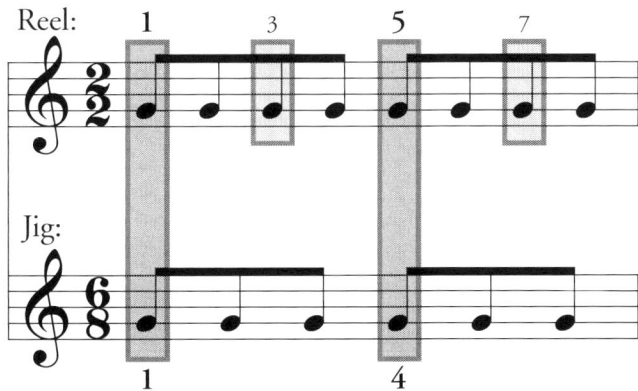

Figure 37. The pulse and its subdivisions in a reel and a jig. The darker shaded areas show the two pulses of the jig and the two primary pulses of the reel. The lighter shaded areas show the two secondary pulses of the reel. Large numbers show the pulse in the jig and the primary pulse in the reel. Slighter numbers show the secondary pulse in the reel.

Develop an Absolutely Dependable Sense of the Pulse

It is one thing to understand that you shouldn't omit an on-pulse note. It is quite another to know, instinctively, which notes those are.

You must develop an absolutely reliable sense of the pulse in the tunes you play. This is the cornerstone of choosing good breathing spots, and, therefore, of playing with flexible and vital phrasing.

A rock-solid sense of the pulse makes breathing choices far simpler. By never omitting on-pulse notes, you narrow the field of potential breathing places by as much as one-half (in reels and hornpipes) or one-third (in jigs, slides, slip jigs and hop jigs). None of the shaded notes in Figure 37 should be omitted. (See previous page.)

If it is difficult for you to sense the pulse of a tune, you may need to work on internalizing the music and feeling its rhythms in your body. Learning to dance to the music is a great way to do this.

Tapping your foot on the pulse helps many players as well.

If you do tap your foot, be sensitive to those around you. If you tap loudly you may be annoying others. If your loud tapping is not rhythmically accurate, there is no doubt that you are annoying others, whether or not they have the nerve to tell you. Tapping your toe inside your shoe can be a good alternative.

Breathing Opportunities Are Often Plentiful

If you are not used to creating breathing places in the manner I've been describing, you may be surprised at how many are indicated in these transcriptions. In most tunes there are more breathing opportunities than you will need, and using them all would make the tune sound too fragmented. As you listen to the CDs that come with this book, you'll hear, for each tune, one example of how I chose to use just a few of these breathing opportunities.

You'll also notice that many tunes have a breathing place indicated very near its beginning. You would breathe there only if you had already played the tune, gone back to the start to repeat it, and then needed some air.

The Breathing Suggestions Are *Only* Suggestions

Remember, breathing choices are subjective, and you may not concur with all of mine. Feel free to create breathing places that feel right to you, within the bounds of the strategies we are discussing in these pages.

As mentioned on p. 10, *300 Gems of Irish Music for All Instruments* contains "blank slate" versions of these tune transcriptions, ones that do *not* include suggestions for breathing, ornamentation or alterations to the register of notes. Using these transcriptions, you can more easily make note of your own breathing ideas.

The Breath Mark

As mentioned on p. 27, the breath mark – ʼ – is widely used in classical music to indicate a place one may take a breath (or for non-wind players, a place to create a brief space in the music). In that tradition, a breath mark is usually placed slightly above the top line of the staff, in between two notes or above a rest. This shows the wind player that she may take a quick breath between the two notes, taking a bit of time away from the end of the first of those notes to do so, or that the rest provides a good place to breathe.

Since it is almost never workable to "sneak" a quick breath this way between two notes of an Irish dance tune, I use the breath mark in a different way.

I place a breath mark directly *above* a notehead to indicate either:

1. that an eighth note can be entirely omitted, or
2. that a note longer than an eighth note can have an eighth-note's worth of time removed *from its beginning* in order to create a breathing space. For an example of this, see Figure 47 on p. 39.

I place a breath mark above and somewhat to the *right* of the notehead to indicate that the note can have an eighth-note's worth of time removed *from its end* in order to create a breathing space.

Below you will find three examples of breathing places created by shortening notes in this way (Figures 39, 40 and 41).

How the Breath Mark Is Used in This Book

1. In the case of an **eighth note** that can be omitted, the breath mark is placed directly over its notehead, as shown below.

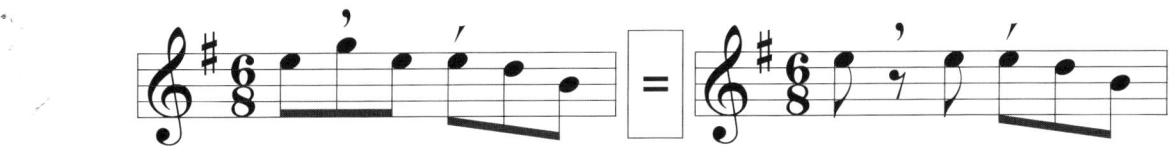

Figure 38. Measure 2 from tune 100, Haste to the Wedding, *showing how an eighth note can be omitted to create a breathing place. **CD #2, track 71.** You will find the complete tune on p. 86.*

2. In the case of a **quarter note** that can be shortened to an eighth note, the breath mark is placed above the midpoint of the duration of the quarter note.

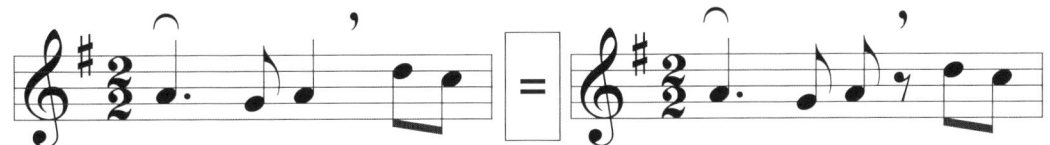

Figure 39. Measure 1 from tune 58, Johnny Going to Céilí, *showing how a quarter note can be shortened to an eighth note to create a breathing place. **CD #2, track 72.** You will find the complete tune on p. 68.*

3. In the case of a **dotted quarter note** that can be shortened to a quarter note, the breath mark is placed at the two-thirds point of the duration of the dotted quarter note.

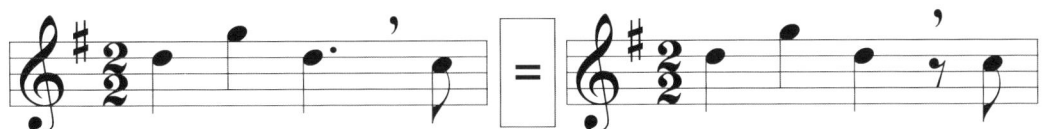

Figure 40. Measure 6 from tune 91, Martin Kirwan's March, *showing how a dotted quarter note can be shortened to a quarter note to create a breathing place. **CD #2, track 73.** You will find the complete tune on p. 79.*

4. In the case of **half notes or longer notes**, the breath mark is placed near the end of that note's duration to indicate shortening that note by one eighth note. Below is an example where a half note is shortened.

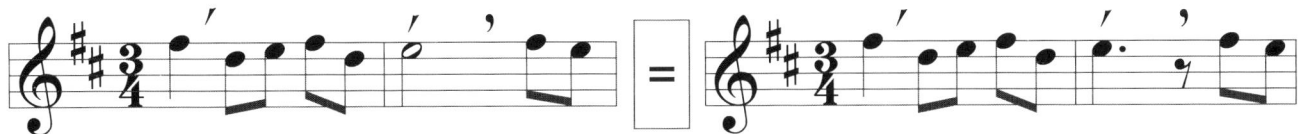

Figure 41. Measures 7 and 8 from the B-part of tune 94, the harp piece Lord Inchiquin, *showing how a half note can be shortened to a dotted quarter note to create a breathing place. **CD #2, track 74.** You will find the complete tune on p. 80.*

I also use the breath mark to indicate where you can alter long rolls, short rolls and cranns to create good breathing spaces. I'll explain this, and show examples, on the following two pages.

Five Breathing Strategies

Below are five strategies for finding and choosing breathing spots. For further discussion of these issues, with more musical examples, see *The Essential Guide to Irish Flute and Tin Whistle* and *The Essential Tin Whistle Toolbox*. (It should be noted, however, that since the publication of those earlier books I have reconfigured the way I organize these breathing strategies. The following is therefore a somewhat revised and updated approach to the subject.)

Breathing Strategy #1: Shortening a Long Note

In all Irish dance tune types (except the polka) the pulse is subdivided into eighth notes. And in most tunes, you will find some notes that are longer than an eighth note.

You can often shorten such longer notes by an increment of one eighth note's duration, using the resulting space for breathing, without disrupting the flow of the tune.

Three examples of this strategy are shown in Figures 39, 40 and 41 on the previous page.

When shortening a dotted quarter note by one eighth note, the breathing place thus created sometimes falls on a pulse. This is one of only two situations I am aware of in which it is appropriate to breathe on a pulse. (For the other, see "Breathing in Slow-Moving Tunes" on p. 42.) In fact, Figure 40, on the previous page, shows an example of this kind of appropriate on-pulse breathing, occurring in that case on the secondary pulse of a march.

Here are two more examples:

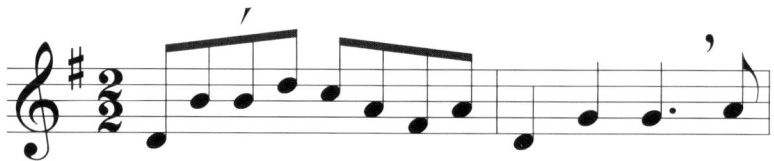

Figure 42. Measures 3 and 4 from tune 77, the hornpipe Kit O'Mahoney's. *The breathing space shown falls on the secondary pulse.* **CD #2, track 75.** *You will find the complete tune on p. 74.*

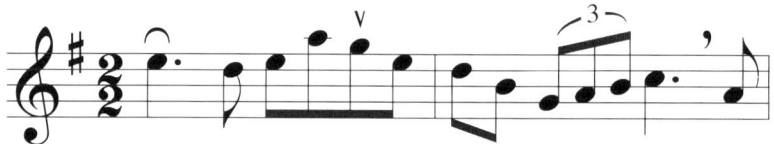

Figure 43. The first two measures of the B-part of tune 122, the set dance An Cúisín Bán. *The breathing space shown falls on the secondary pulse.* **CD #2, track 76.** *You will find the complete tune on p. 95.*

Breathing Strategy #2: Breaking a Long Roll

This strategy works only when the first note of the long roll is an *on-pulse* note. In these cases, the second note of the roll, by necessity, falls on a weaker, off-pulse beat, no matter what type of tune you are playing. The second note of such a roll can therefore be omitted without disrupting the flow of the music.

Of course, when you do this you no longer have a roll, so you can use whatever articulations you like with the notes that remain.

Here is an example:

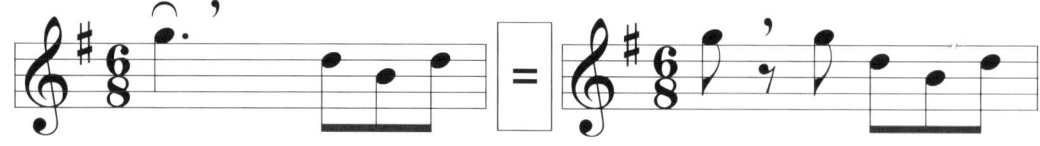

Figure 44. Breaking the long roll in the first measure of the B-part of tune 27, The High Part of the Road. **CD #2, track 77.** *You will find the complete tune on p. 58.*

If you try this technique with a long roll that begins on an *off-pulse* beat, you will quickly hear why it doesn't work. For an example, take a look at Figure 45.

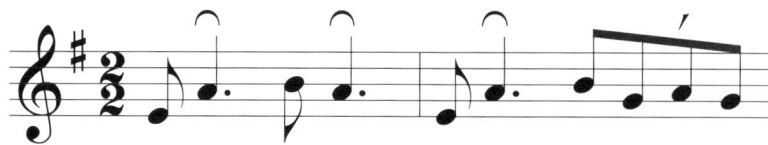

Figure 45. The first two measures of tune 40, the reel The Maids of Mt. Kisco. *You will find the complete tune on p. 63.*

These long rolls begin on weak, off-pulse beats (eighth-note beats 2 or 6 in this case). If you leave out the middle note of any one of them, as shown in the example below, there will be no sound occurring on the secondary pulse (eighth-note beats 3 or 7). This produces an odd "hiccuping" effect. A better example of inarticulate breathing in traditional Irish music could hardly be found.

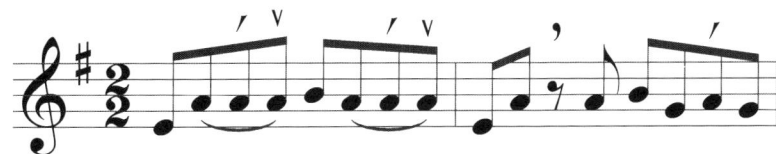

Figure 46. The first two measures of tune 40, The Maids of Mt. Kisco, *showing an example of inarticulate breathing in measure 2 produced by breaking a long roll that begins on an off-pulse beat. The long rolls in measure 1 are shown in exploded view. Breaking either of them would produce the same distracting effect.* **CD #2, track 78.**

BREATHING STRATEGY #3: TRUNCATING A LONG ROLL

Here is a breathing strategy that works *only* with the type of long roll we just encountered in Figures 45 and 46: long rolls that begin on weak or off-pulse beats. By omitting either the first or third eighth note of such long rolls, you can create a good breathing spot. The two eighth notes that remain can be played as a short roll, or simply as two repeated eighth notes.

Again using *The Maids of Mt. Kisco* to illustrate, here are two examples:

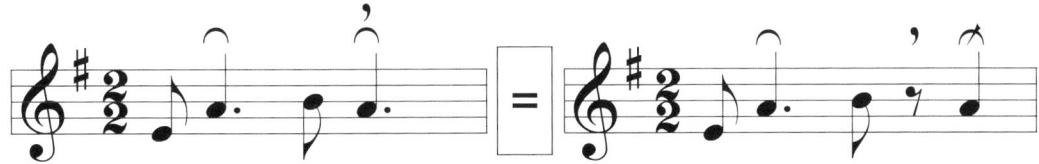

Figure 47. The first measure of The Maids of Mt. Kisco *with a breathing place created by omitting the first note of a long roll that begins on an off-pulse beat. In this case, a short roll remains. Note the location of the breath mark, directly above the long roll symbol.* **CD #2, track 79.**

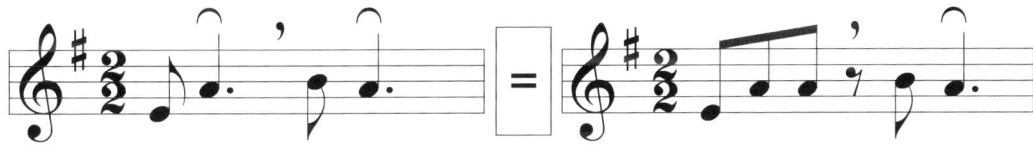

Figure 48. The first measure of The Maids of Mt. Kisco *with a breathing place created by omitting the last note of a long roll that begins on an off-pulse beat. Note the location of the breath mark, two-thirds of the way through the long roll.* **CD #2, track 80.**

BREATHING STRATEGY #4: TRUNCATING A SHORT ROLL

Short rolls almost always begin on a strong, on-pulse beat. You may often omit the second eighth note of such short rolls in order to create a good breathing opportunity. An example appears below.

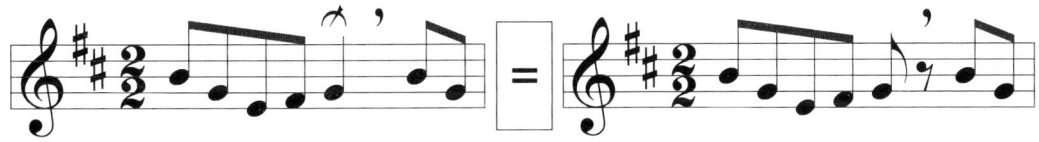

Figure 49. The first measure of tune 68, the reel Drogheda Bay, *with a breathing place created by omitting the second note of a short roll.* **CD #2, track 81.** *You will find the complete tune on p. 71.*

Breathing Strategy #5: Omitting a Nonessential Eighth Note

Most eighth notes are essential to the spirit and shape of a tune, but some are not. Such nonessential eighth notes can often be entirely omitted with no loss to the integrity of the tune. Their omission can in fact become a refreshing variation. In such instances, listeners often don't notice that anything is being omitted, or that a breath is even occurring. They are enjoying the well-shaped phrasing that is caressing their ears or urging on their dancing feet and they feel no disruption to the flow of the music.

As discussed earlier, eighth notes that fall on the primary or secondary pulse in dance tunes are by nature emphasized and must not be omitted. It follows then that nonessential eighth notes always fall on off-pulse beats. Here is an example:

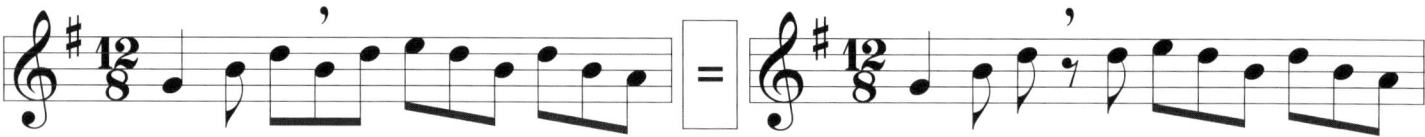

Figure 50. Measure 3 of tune 121, the slide or set dance O'Connell's Farewell to Dublin, *with a breathing place created by omitting a nonessential eighth note.* **CD #2, track 82.** *You will find the complete tune on p. 95.*

A variant on this strategy occurs when there are two sixteenth notes (which, taken together, equal the duration of one eighth note) that can be omitted to create a breathing place. In such a case, you omit both the sixteenth notes. Figure 51 shows how this is notated, and Figure 52 shows how it sounds.

Figure 51. The first four bars of the C-part of tune 15, the jig Tell Her I Am. *Note the breath mark over a sixteenth note in the second measure. You will find the complete tune on p. 53.*

Figure 52. The first four bars of the C-part of Tell Her I Am *with a breathing place created by omitting two sixteenth notes.* **CD #2, track 83.**

You'll find this kind of breathing opportunity in tunes 7, 13, 15, 19, 27 and 99.

Breathing Within Triplets in Hornpipes

In hornpipes we often find eighth-note triplets, and it seems they always begin on a primary or secondary pulse. When omitting off-pulse notes from such a triplet, most players omit both the second and third notes. You may omit just the second note if you feel that gives you enough time for an ample breath.

Let's take a look at an example from tune 73, *O'Callaghan's*. Figure 53 shows how this breathing strategy is notated and Figure 54 shows how it sounds.

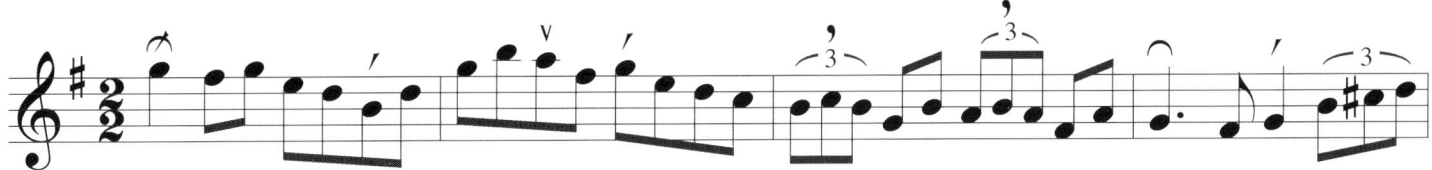

Figure 53. The last four measures of the A-part of tune 73, O'Callaghan's. *Note the breath indications within the eighth-note triplets in the third measure. You will find the complete tune on p. 73.*

Figure 54. The last four measures of the A-part of tune 73, O'Callaghan's.
*You may omit both the second and third notes of eighth-note triplets for breathing purposes.
When playing the tune, you would normally choose only one of these two breathing opportunities.* **CD #2, track 84.**

When omitting the second and third notes of such a triplet, you can, if you wish, play the first (remaining) note as a quarter note instead of as an eighth note, taking a breath where the final eighth note of the triplet would have been.

THE SPECIAL CASE OF POLKAS

Polkas are usually notated in 2/4 time. This means there are two quarter-note pulses per measure. Each quarter-note pulse is then subdivided into four sixteenth notes. The shortest customary rhythmic unit in a polka is therefore usually represented as a sixteenth note, whereas with all other tune types it is usually represented as an eighth note.

So far, we have looked at creating breathing spaces that are each one eighth note in duration. With polkas, however, the breathing spaces can either be one sixteenth note or one eighth note in duration.

A polka's sixteenth note may, depending upon the speed of the tune, allow you enough time to get a good breath. If it doesn't, you could omit two sixteenth notes or an eighth note. Or, you can catch a partial breath by omitting the sixteenth note and then start looking for another breathing opportunity right away.

In tune 88, *Din Tarrant's* (see below), I have indicated breathing suggestions of both the sixteenth and eighth note variety. Figure 55 shows how they are notated and Figure 56 shows how they sound.

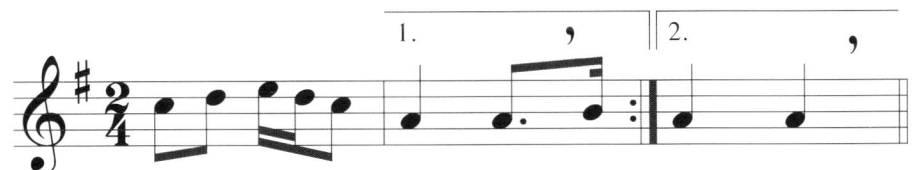

Figure 55. Measures 7-9 of tune 88, the polka Din Tarrant's, *with two suggested breathing indications.
You will find the complete tune on p. 78.*

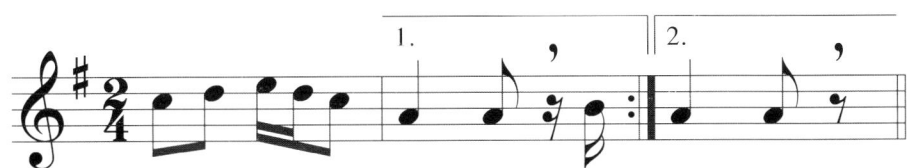

Figure 56. The same measures as in Figure 55, above. Here we see how two breathing places are created by omitting first a sixteenth note, and then an eighth note. **CD #2, track 85.**

Breathing in Slow-Moving Tunes

In slow-moving tunes it sometimes feels quite natural to allow yourself an entire quarter note of space for breathing. In the transcription of tune 150, *Down the Hill* (see p. 111), most of the breath marks indicate eighth-note breathing spaces. But others indicate that a quarter note can be a more appropriate duration for a breath. Figure 57 shows how these breathing opportunities are notated, and Figure 58 shows how they sound.

Figure 57. Measures 5-8 of the B-part of tune 150, Down the Hill, *with two suggested breathing indications. You will find the complete tune on p. 111.*

Figure 58. The same measures as in Figure 57, above. Here we see how the two breathing places are created by omitting first a quarter note and then an eighth note. Of course, you would not use both breathing places. **CD #2, track 86.**

Note that the first breathing place shown in both Figures 57 and 58 falls upon the second pulse in the ¾ metric pattern. This is normally the weakest of the three pulses. This illustrates one of only two situations I am aware of in which it is appropriate to breathe on the pulse. (For the other, see "Breathing Strategy #1: Shortening a Long Note" on p. 38.)

Breathing at the End of a Part

An A-part or B-part of a tune will often end in a way that presents a clear opportunity for a breathing spot. Figure 59, below, shows an example.

Figure 59. From tune 1, Have a Drink with Me, *the last two measures of the first A-part and the first two measures of its repeat. A breath is shown near the end of the first A-part.* **CD #2, track 87.** *You will find the complete tune on p. 48.*

You'll come across many tunes that suggest this kind of phrasing. But instead of automatically taking a breath at the end of the part, you might choose instead to keep playing and carry the energy on through into its repeat or into the next part of the tune.

Figure 60. The same excerpt as above. This time a breath is taken well into the repeat of the A-part instead of at the end of the first A-part. The momentum is carried through into the repeat of the part. **CD #2, track 88.**

Don't Let Breathing Interfere With Natural Musical Contours or Forward Motion

There are plenty of times when breathing according to one of these strategies will nevertheless disrupt the tune. This is because certain notes are needed to define the natural contours of the melody or to help maintain its forward motion.

For an illustration, let's look at the first two measures of *The Farewell Reel*.

Figure 61. The first two measures of tune 48, The Farewell Reel. *You will find the complete tune on p. 65.*

Below is an example of inarticulate breathing in this tune excerpt. The last note of the first measure is omitted, an off-pulse note that might at first seem to serve simply as a connecting note.

*Figure 62. The same excerpt, showing an example of inarticulate breathing. CD #2, **track 89.***

In fact, the note that has been omitted is an essential one (at least I think so), even though it might at first seem to fit the description of strategy #5 (omitting a nonessential eighth note). I find its omission to be disruptive of the downward sweep and forward motion of the melody.

If you want to breathe somewhere in these measures, I think you would do better to choose one of the two options shown below in Figures 63 and 64.

*Figure 63. An example of an articulate breathing spot created by shortening a quarter note. CD #2, **track 90.***

*Figure 64. Another example of an articulate breathing spot, this one created by omitting a nonessential eighth note in the second measure. CD #2, **track 91.***

The Note After a Breath May Function in a New Way

When you omit or shorten a note in order to take a breath, the note that comes after the breath feels different. That note is now the beginning of a new musical thought or phrase, whereas before it was a note in the midst of a phrase.

The space created by a breath functions like a punctuation mark. You may choose to play the note after the breath in a different way, since it now serves a different function. You might even play a different pitch altogether, one that does a better or different kind of job of starting your new musical thought.

New Insights, New Challenges

Having read these pages, you might now listen to your favorite flute and whistle players with new insight into their phrasing and breathing. You may not have realized they were shortening notes and leaving notes out. Notice how frequently they breathe. You may not be able to hear the actual sound of their breathing, but you can observe where they are creating space for it.

If you are not used to shortening and omitting notes, start trying it out. You may make mistakes for a while. When you create a breathing spot in an inappropriate place, simply notice how that feels and sounds and don't judge yourself harshly. Such "mistakes" are golden learning opportunities. Let them help you.

With enough time and practice, these breathing strategies will become second nature.

A Closer Look: Phrasing Within Phrases

The phrases I have been writing about here – all of the notes that come between two breathing spaces – can be thought of as large phrases.

Within a large phrase, you can further sculpt the music into smaller groupings and flows of notes. These sub-phrases relate to one another much as words interact within a spoken phrase.

We can define and shape these sub-phrases by using the following techniques:

- changes in the weight, flow, and pulse of the breath
- changes in loudness
- changes in tone color
- changes in the qualities of lilt
- finger articulations (cuts and strikes)
- breath articulations (tonguing and throating)
- pitch inflections (fingered slides or breath slides)
- breath vibrato
- finger vibrato
- choices of how or whether to emphasize the pulse at any given moment

Perhaps you can add to this list.

To further explore this expanded view of phrasing, see *The Essential Guide to Irish Flute and Tin Whistle* or *The Essential Tin Whistle Toolbox*, particularly the parts that compare music to spoken language.

Section One

Section One: Flute-Friendly Tunes

The bulk of the tunes in this collection are "flute-friendly," tunes which favor the flute's natural capabilities while steering clear of its limitations.

Note that flute-friendly tunes fit well on the tin whistle and uilleann pipes as well.

Many of these tunes were no doubt made by players of Irish flute, uilleann pipes and tin whistle, the three simple-system wind instruments of traditional Irish music. Others seem to be more idiomatic to non-wind instruments, but nevertheless meet the following flute-friendly criteria:

- The tunes fall within the comfortable octave-plus-a-sixth range of the standard Irish flute, never venturing below low D or above high B.

- The tunes flow naturally under a flute player's fingers, and present no special fingering challenges.

- The tunes do not include frequent and/or rapid jumps from the high register down to the low, a maneuver which can be challenging on the flute (but doesn't seem to be for the high D whistle).

- The only notes that occur in these tunes are D, E, F♯, G, A, B, C♮ and C♯, the notes that are easily played by completely covering and uncovering the Irish flute's six finger holes. The tunes do not contain notes that require cross-fingerings (with the exception of C♮), half-hole fingerings, or the use of metal keys.

- The notes that most naturally invite ornamentation are the ones that Irish flute players can embellish with variety and ease: namely E, F♯, G, A and B – and not C♮ or C♯.

Since the crann on D (and E) can be challenging for all but the advanced flute player, it could not be considered a flute-friendly technique. However, because cranns are such a beautiful element of flute ornamentation, I include five tunes in Section One that call for their use (numbers 29, 30, 71, 72 and 92). Cranns were adopted by Irish flute and whistle players at least as early as 1925, and probably earlier. For players who are not yet comfortable with playing cranns, there are melodic alternatives that can be employed. See pp. 22-23 for information on these.

Section One contains 30 jigs, 42 reels, 11 hornpipes, 2 slip jigs, 1 hop jig, 2 polkas, 2 slides, 1 march, 1 set dance and 2 harp pieces.

Flute-Friendly Tunes   *Jigs*

1. Have a Drink with Me

CD 1, Track 1

2. Slieve Russell

CD 1, Track 2

3. Hardiman's Fancy

CD 1, Track 3

12. The Humours of Trim

CD 1, Track 12

Note: C-sharps can be played as C-naturals, or as a pitch in between C-natural and C-sharp.

13. The Lark on the Strand

CD 1, Track 13

14. Munster Bacon

CD 1, Track 14

15. Tell Her I Am, three-part version

CD 1, Track 15

16. Tell Her I Am, two-part version

based on a 2008 session recording with
Connie O'Connell (fiddle) and Peadar Ó Riada (concertina)

CD 1, Track 16

17. A Tailor I Am

based on a 2008 session recording with
Connie O'Connell (fiddle) and Peadar Ó Riada (concertina)

CD 1, Track 17

18. The Wandering Minstrel

based on a 2008 session recording with
Connie O'Connell (fiddle) and Peadar Ó Riada (concertina)

CD 1, Track 18

Flute-Friendly Tunes — 54 — Jigs

22. Hudie Gallagher's March

based on the playing of Francie and Mickey Byrne (fiddles)
on the late 1970s recording "Ceol na dTéad"

CD 1, Track 22

23. Down the Back Lane

based on the playing of Paddy Canny (fiddle)
on the 1955 recording "Traditional Fiddle Music from East Clare"

CD 1, Track 23

Flute-Friendly Tunes   56   Jigs

24. Tongs by the Fire

CD 1, Track 24

25. Top of Cork Road

CD 1, Track 25

26. I Ne'er Shall Wean Her

CD 1, Track 26

27. The High Part of the Road

28. Trip to Killavil

29. Fraher's Jig

30. Strike the Gay Harp

CD 1, Track 30

Flute-Friendly Tunes

Reels

31. Sword in Hand

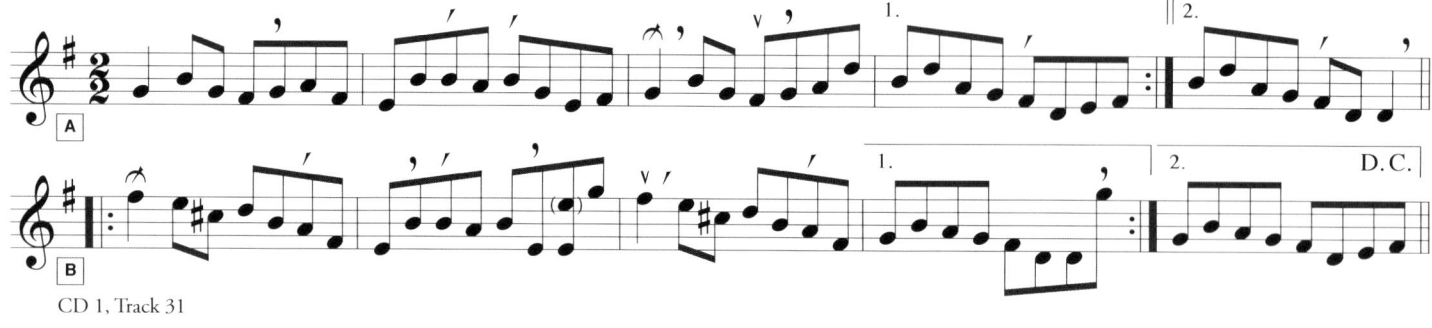

CD 1, Track 31

32. The Virginia Reel

CD 1, Track 32

33. Sailing Into Walpole's Marsh

based on the playing of Andy Irvine (bouzouki), Paul Brady (guitar) and Kevin Burke (fiddle) on the 1976 recording "Andy Irvine Paul Brady"

CD 1, Track 33

34. The Queen of May

CD 1, Track 34

35. Toss the Feathers

CD 1, Track 35

36. The Earl's Chair

CD 1, Track 36

37. The Chattering Magpie

CD 1, Track 37

38. The Monaghan Twig

CD 1, Track 38

39. Jackson's Reel

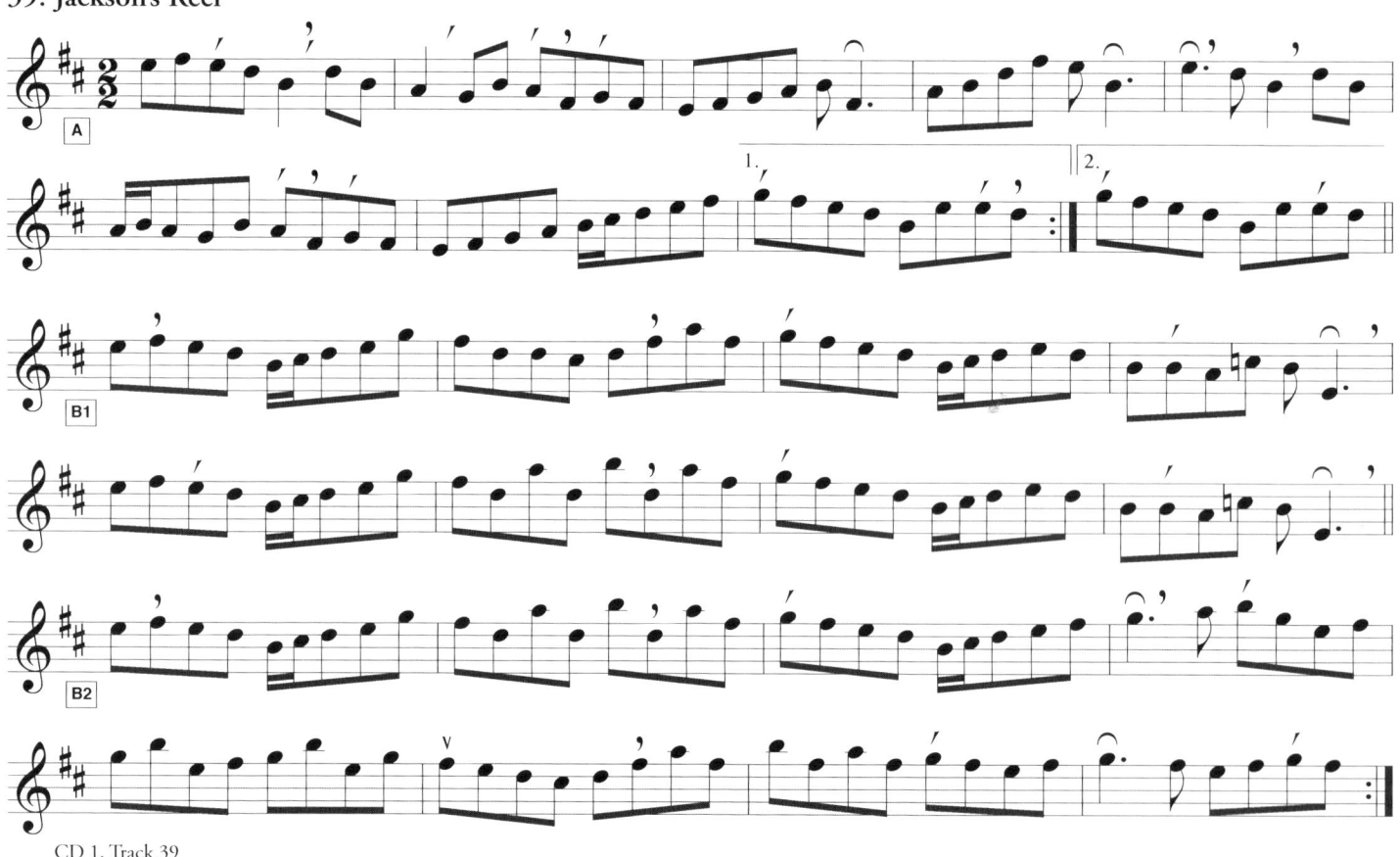

CD 1, Track 39

43. The Galway Rambler

44. The Connaught Heifers

45. The Longford Tinker

based on a Bothy Band live recording from the 1970s
Matt Molloy (flute), Paddy Keenan (uilleann pipes), Kevin Burke (fiddle)

CD 1, Track 43

CD 1, Track 44

CD 1, Track 45

Flute-Friendly Tunes   64   Reels

50. Killarney Boys of Pleasure

CD 1, Track 50

51. The Corner House

CD 1, Track 51

52. The Windy Gap

CD 1, Track 52

53. The Reel with the Birl

CD 1, Track 53

54. Ríl Phadaí 'n Atharaigh (Paddy from Agharagh)

based on the playing of Francie and Mickey Byrne (fiddles) on the late 1970s recording "Ceol na dTéad"

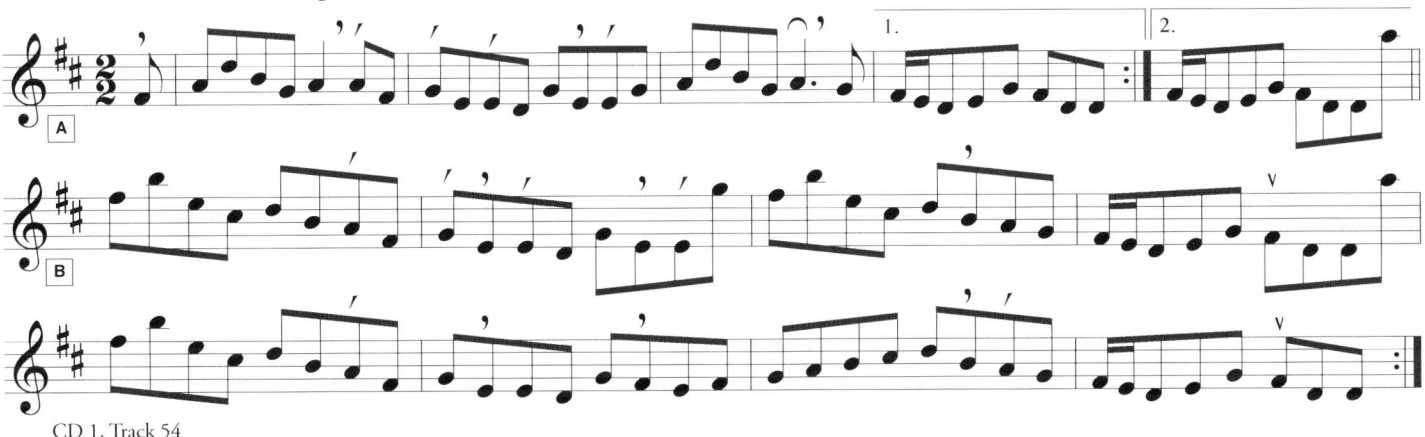

CD 1, Track 54

55. Lady Gordon

based on the playing of Gearóid Ó hAllmhuráin (concertina) and Patrick Ourceau (fiddle) on the 1999 recording "Tracin'"

CD 1, Track 55

56. Maud Miller

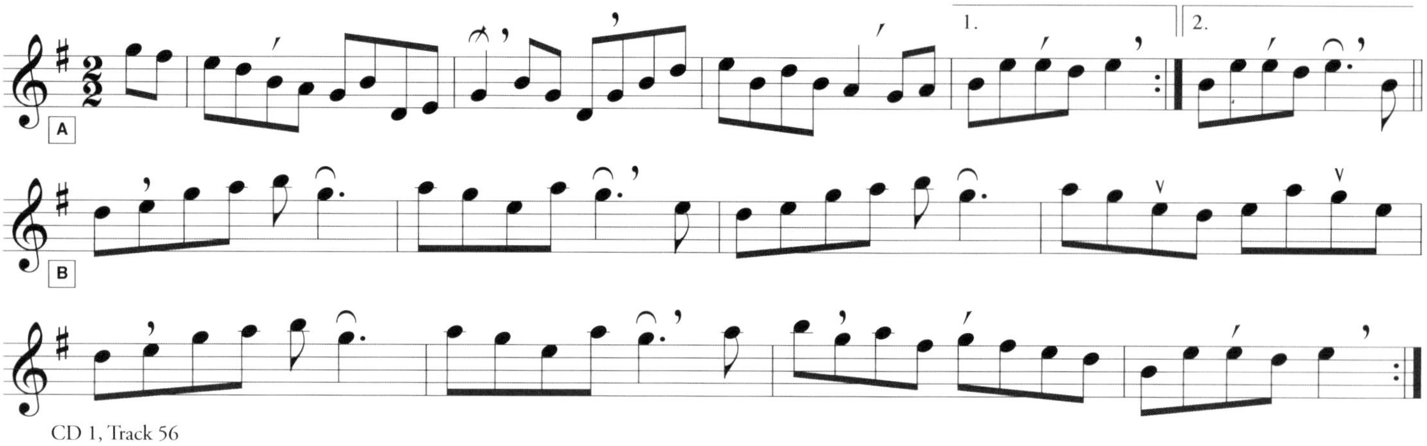

CD 1, Track 56

57. The Crooked Road to Dublin

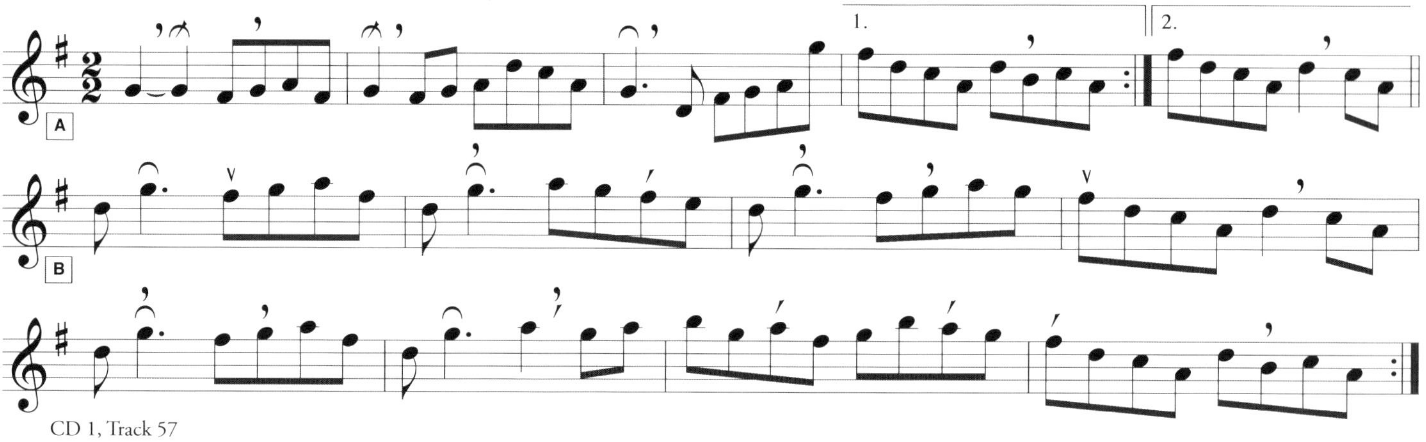

CD 1, Track 57

58. Johnny Going to Céilí

CD 1, Track 58

59. The Sailor's Bonnet

CD 1, Track 59

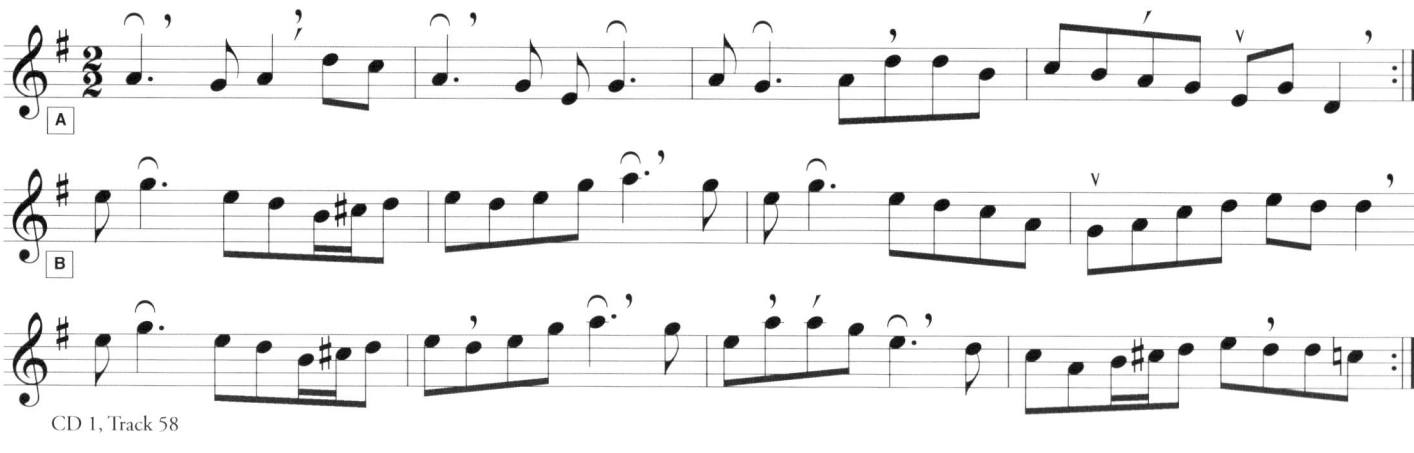

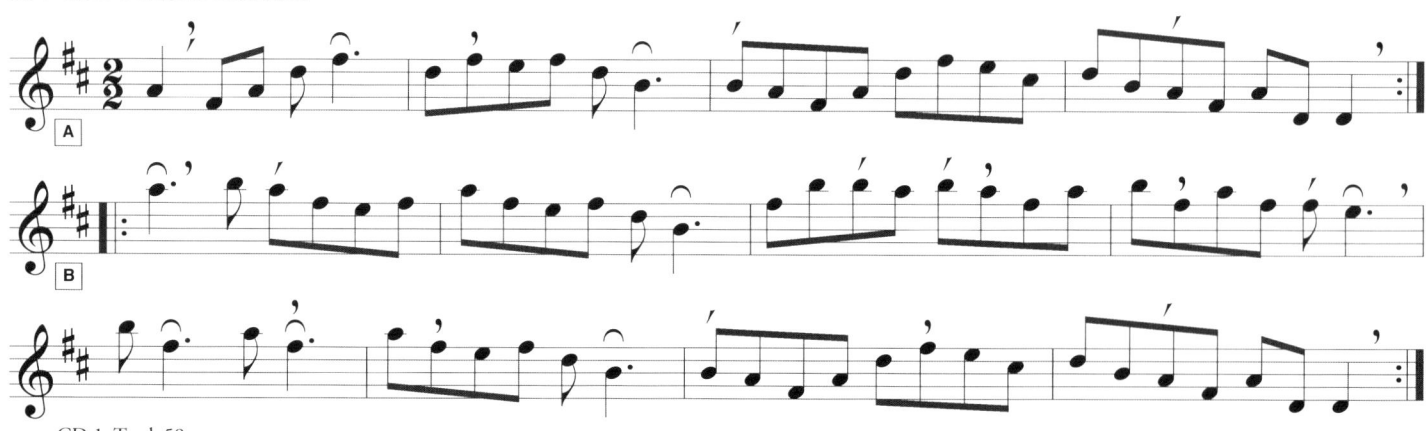

70. The Old High Reel

CD 1, Track 70

71. McDonagh's

CD 1, Track 71

72. George White's Favorite

CD 1, Track 72

Flute-Friendly Tunes

Hornpipes

73. O'Callaghan's

74. The Blackbird

75. Boys of Ballycastle

CD 1, Track 73

CD 1, Track 74

CD 1, Track 75

82. Fitzgerald's

based on the playing of Paddy Cronin (fiddle)
on his 78 rpm recording from 1950

CD 1, Track 82

83. Tuamgraney Castle

CD 1, Track 83

Flute-Friendly Tunes   76   Hornpipes

Flute-Friendly Tunes — Other Tune Types

84. I'm the Boy for Bewitching Them · *Slip Jig*

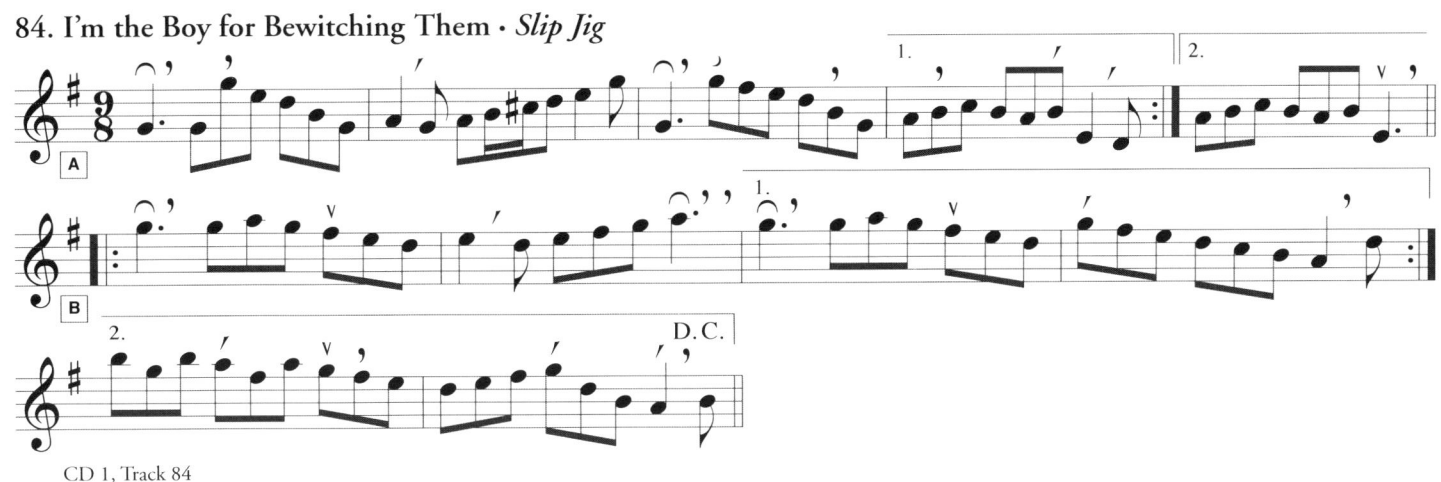

85. The Ship Doctor · *Slip Jig*

alternately titled "The Hyp-Doctor" in John Johnson's *Choice Collection of 200 Favourite Country Dances,* vol. 5 (1750)

86. My Mind Will Never Be Easy · *Hop Jig*

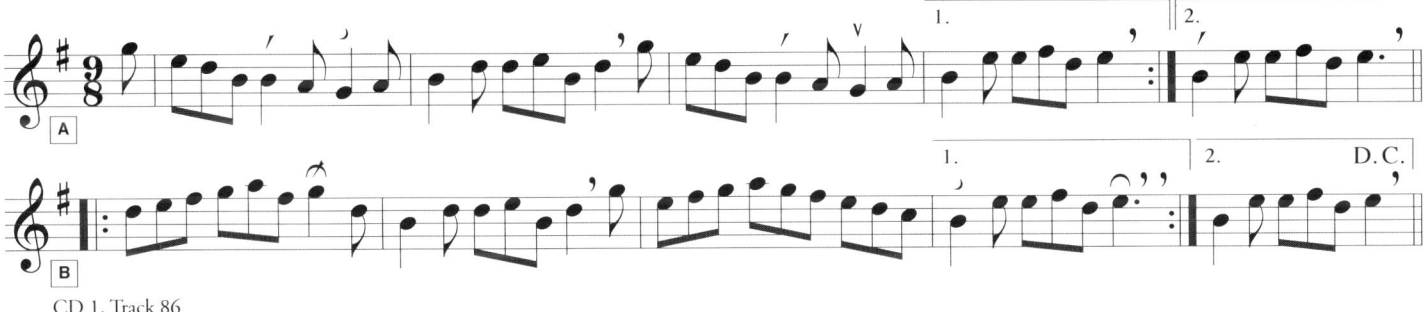

87. Ballydesmond Polka #1

88. Din Tarrant's · *Polka*

based on the playing of Dennis Doody (button accordion)
on the 1978 recording "Kerry Music"

CD 1, Track 88

89. Pádraig O'Keeffe's · *Slide*

based on the playing of Dennis Murphy (fiddle) on the recording
"Music from Sliabh Luachra," made between 1948 and 1969

CD 1, Track 89

90. Get Up Old Woman and Shake Yourself · *Slide*

CD 1, Track 90

91. Martin Kirwan's March

based on the playing of Lucy Farr (fiddle) on the 1991 recording "Heart and Home"

CD 1, Track 91

92. The Blackbird · *Set Dance*

CD 1, Track 92

This tune is usually played in a rhythm similar to that of a hornpipe.

93. George Brabazon · *Harp Piece*

Turlough O'Carolan (1670-1738)

CD 1, Track 93

Flute-Friendly Tunes   Other Tune Types

94. Lord Inchiquin · *Harp Piece* Turlough O'Carolan (1670-1738)

CD 1, Track 94

Section Two

Section Two: Tunes of Non-Wind Origin

These are tunes which I believe originated with players of non-wind instruments such as fiddle, accordion, concertina, tenor banjo and harp.

- Most of these tunes have notes that fall below the low D of the standard Irish flute and require the player to make creative adjustments to the melody. Such too-low notes (and sometimes other notes that precede and/or follow them) have been raised by an octave in these tune settings. The original low notes are represented by open, stemless diamond-shaped noteheads. (See pp. 27-28 for more on this.)

- Some tunes require the player to jump frequently and/or rapidly from the high register down to the low, a maneuver which can be challenging on the flute but presents no special difficulty for non-wind instruments. It also does not seem to be challenging on the high D whistle.

- Many tunes contain sequences of fingerings that are idiomatic to their instrument of origin but which fall less naturally on the flute (as well as whistle and uilleann pipes).

- The only notes that occur in these tunes are D, E, F♯, G, A, B, C♮ and C♯, the notes that are easily played by completely covering and uncovering the Irish flute's six finger holes. These tunes do not contain notes that require cross-fingerings (with the exception of C♮), half-hole fingerings, or the use of metal keys.

- Many of these tunes invite ornamentation on C and C♯. These notes are not as readily ornamented on the flute as on non-wind instruments. When long or short rolls on C or C♯ would likely be played on other instruments, the flute player can either play unadorned notes or employ melodic variation, finger or breath vibrato, and shadings of pitch, tone and loudness. (There are fingerings that allow flute players to simulate rolls on C and C♯. For information on these, see *The Essential Guide to Irish Flute and Tin Whistle* or *The Essential Tin Whistle Toolbox*.)

Section Two contains 9 jigs, 12 reels, 4 hornpipes, 1 polka, 1 set dance, and 1 tune that is considered to be both a slide and a set dance.

Tunes of Non-Wind Origin

Jigs

95. The Orphan

CD 2, Track 1

For a low A flute setting of this tune, refer to p. 121 and CD 2, track 98.

96. The Cordal Jig

CD 2, Track 2

97. Paddy's Resource

CD 2, Track 3

98. Vincent Campbell's

based on the playing of Matt Molloy (flute) and Seán Keane (fiddle) on the 1985 recording "Contentment Is Wealth"

CD 2, Track 4

99. Bush on the Hill

CD 2, Track 5

Tunes of Non-Wind Origin   Jigs

103. The Gold Ring

CD 2, Track 9

Tunes of Non-Wind Origin

Reels

104. The Humours of Loughrea

CD 2, Track 10

105. Down the Broom

CD 2, Track 11

106. Fred Finn's

CD 2, Track 12

107. Music in the Glen

CD 2, Track 13

108. Miss Patterson's Slipper

CD 2, Track 14

For a low A flute setting of this tune, refer to p. 122 and CD 2, track 99.

109. The Galtee Reel

CD 2, Track 15

110. Miss McLeod's Reel — based on the playing of Michael J. Kennedy (melodeon in G)

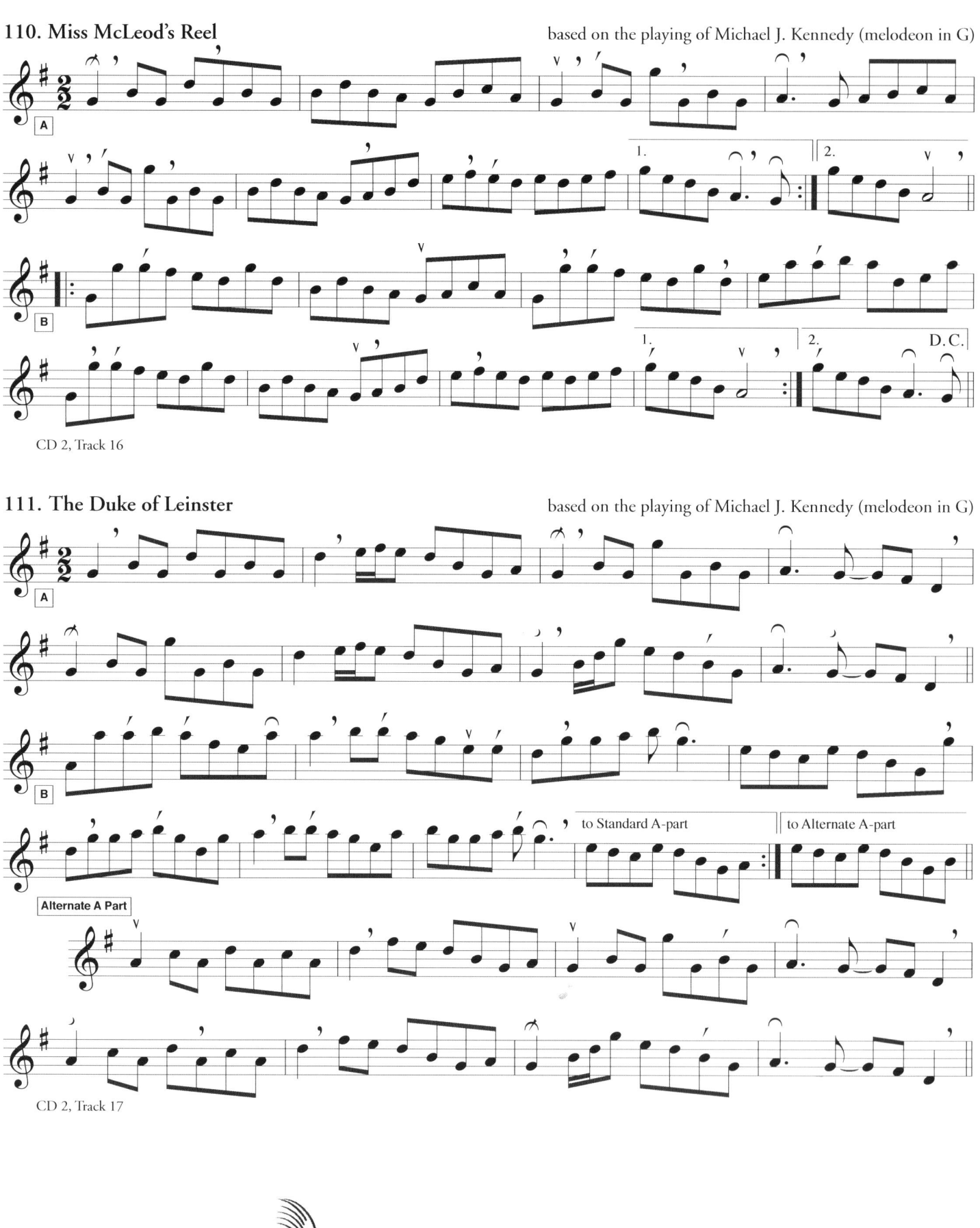

CD 2, Track 16

111. The Duke of Leinster — based on the playing of Michael J. Kennedy (melodeon in G)

CD 2, Track 17

115. The Green Hills of Tyrol

A1

A2

B1

B2

CD 2, Track 21

Tunes of Non-Wind Origin 92 Reels

Tunes of Non-Wind Origin *Hornpipes*

116. Kitty's Wedding — based on the playing of Paddy Cronin (fiddle) on his 78 rpm recording of c. 1952

CD 2, Track 22

117. Jack O'Neill's Fancy

CD 2, Track 23

118. The Pride of Petravore — Percy French (1854-1924)

CD 2, Track 24

119. Madam If You Please

CD 2, Track 25

Tunes of Non-Wind Origin — Hornpipes

Tunes of Non-Wind Origin

Other Tune Types

120. Blackwater Polka #2

based on the playing of Dennis Doody (button accordion)
on the 1978 recording "Kerry Music"

CD 2, Track 26

121. O'Connell's Farewell to Dublin · *Slide and Set Dance*

based on the playing of Patrick Kelly (fiddle)
on the 1978 recording "Ceol an Cláir"

CD 2, Track 27

122. An Cúisín Bán (The White Cushion) · *Set Dance*

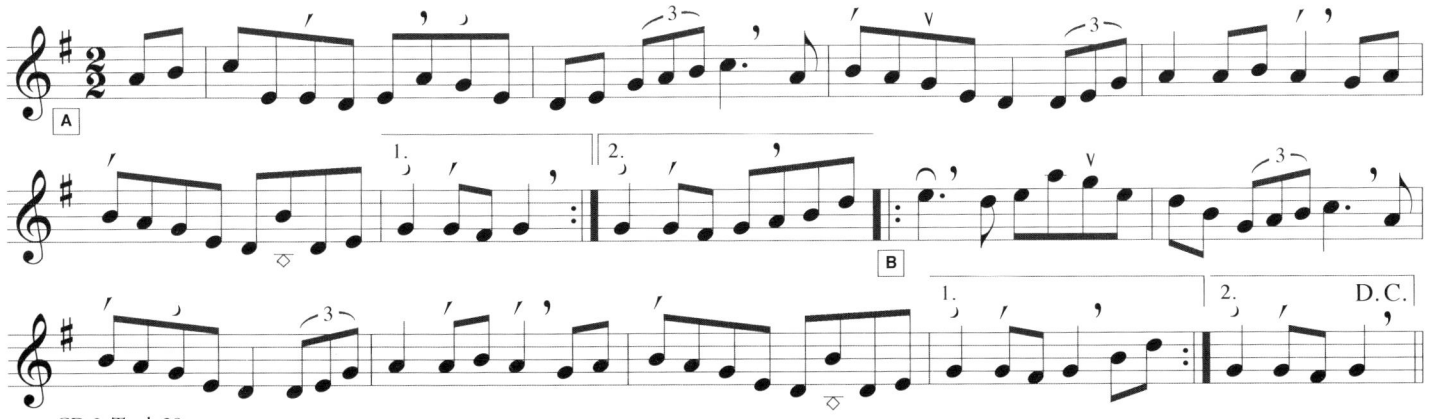

CD 2, Track 28
This tune is usually played in a rhythm similar to that of a hornpipe.

Section Three

Section Three: Tunes Requiring the Use of Keys

These are tunes which employ one or more of the four pitches – E♭, F♮, G♯ and B♭ – that fall outside the natural scale of the Irish, or simple-system wooden flute. For players of wooden Irish flutes, these tunes require the use of one or more metal keys. Players of the modern, Boehm-system flute are typically accustomed to playing these notes, but that is often not the case with players of Irish flute.

It is not physically difficult to use the keys on keyed Irish flutes. It may seem challenging at first, but usually this is only due to unfamiliarity. With experience and practice, it becomes quite natural to use them. Doing so allows the player to open a door to a new body of music, to play tunes many of which I think sound especially lovely on the flute.

Not surprisingly, nearly all tunes of this type originated with players of non-wind instruments.

- Some of these tunes have notes that fall below the low D of the standard Irish flute and require the player to make creative adjustments. Such too-low notes (and sometimes other notes that precede and/or follow them) have been raised by an octave in these tune settings. The original low notes are represented by open, stemless diamond-shaped noteheads. (See pp. 27-28 for more on this.)

- Some tunes require the player to jump frequently and/or rapidly from the high register down to the low, a maneuver which can be challenging on the flute but presents no special difficulty for non-wind instruments. It also does not seem to be challenging on the high D whistle.

- Many tunes contain sequences of fingerings that are idiomatic to their non-wind instrument of origin but which fall less naturally on the flute (as well as whistle and uilleann pipes).

- Many of these tunes invite ornamentation on C and C♯. These notes are not as readily ornamented on the flute as on non-wind instruments. When long or short rolls on C or C♯ would likely be played on other instruments, the flute player can either play unadorned notes or employ melodic variation, finger or breath vibrato, and shadings of pitch, tone and loudness. (There are fingerings that allow flute players to simulate rolls on C and C♯. For information on these, see *The Essential Guide to Irish Flute and Tin Whistle* or *The Essential Tin Whistle Toolbox*.)

- These tunes are often in modes that for the most part cannot be played on Irish flute without the use of keys. These modes include D Dorian, G Dorian, D Aeolian, G Aeolian, F Ionian, C Ionian, A Ionian and G Mixolydian.

Section Three contains 9 jigs, 12 reels, 4 hornpipes, 1 slide, 1 mazurka, and 1 air.

Tunes Requiring the Use of Keys

Jigs

123. The Hag's Purse

CD 2, Track 29

124. An Buachaill Dreoite (The Spent Boy)

based on the playing of the Mulcahy Family on the 2000 recording "The Mulcahy Family"
Michelle Mulcahy (concertina), Louise Mulcahy (uilleann pipes) and Mick Mulcahy (concertina)

CD 2, Track 30

125. The Banks of Glenloe

CD 2, Track 31

126. **The Gallowglass**

based on the playing of Paddy Canny (fiddle)
on the 1955 recording "Traditional Fiddle Music from East Clare"

127. **The Luck Penny**

based on the playing of Paddy Canny (fiddle)
on the 1955 recording "Traditional Fiddle Music from East Clare"

CD 2, Track 32

CD 2, Track 33

Tunes Requiring the Use of Keys   101   Jigs

131. Strop the Razor

CD 2, Track 37

For a high G flute setting of this tune, refer to p. 116 and CD 2, track 94.

135. The Maids of Mitchellstown

CD 2, Track 41

For a low C flute setting of this tune, refer to p. 118 and CD 2, track 95.

136. The Girl That Broke My Heart

CD 2, Track 42

137. The Humours of Scariff

CD 2, Track 43

138. My Maryanne

CD 2, Track 44

For a low C flute setting of this tune, refer to p. 119 and CD 2, track 96.

139. The Big Reel of Ballynacally

CD 2, Track 45

140. The Tempest

CD 2, Track 46

147. Early in the Morning

CD 2, Track 53

Tunes Requiring the Use of Keys — Hornpipes

Tunes Requiring the Use of Keys — *Other Tune Types*

148. The Man From Glauntaun · *Slide*

based on the playing of Dennis Doody (button accordion)
on the 1978 recording "Kerry Music"

CD 2, Track 54

For a high G flute setting of this tune, refer to p. 115 and CD 2, track 93.

149. John Doherty's Mazurka

based on the playing of Altan on the 1993 recording "Island Angel"
Mairéad Ní Mhaonaigh (fiddle), Frankie Kennedy (flute), Dermot Byrne (accordion)

CD 2, Track 55

150. Down the Hill • *Air*

CD 2, Track 56

Tunes Requiring the Use of Keys

Other Tune Types

Appendix: Playing Tunes on Non-D Flutes

Simple-system flutes can be found in a variety of pitch levels, or keys. Why might you play Irish tunes on a flute pitched higher or lower than the standard D flute? Here are three reasons:

1. **For the pleasure of a new sound and feel.** When you use D flute fingerings on a flute pitched higher or lower than D, the tune moves into a nonstandard key and there is a shift of mood, timbre and sensation.
2. **To play along with instruments that are pitched higher or lower than D.** For example, to play with an uilleann piper who is using a flat set pitched in B, you might use a flute that is also pitched in (low) B. Both players use their normal D instrument fingerings and the tune comes out sounding lower than it would sound on standard D instruments. As mentioned above, the mood, timbre and sensation also shift.
3. **To play in modal scales which include one or more of the four notes - E♭, F♮, G♯ and B♭ - that fall outside the D flute's natural scale.** Here the goal is to play the tune at its *standard* pitch level, along with normally-pitched fiddles, accordions, pipes, etc. You can do this using a keyed D flute, but you can also play many of these tunes on keyless flutes pitched in A, C, E, F or G, using fingerings that are different from those you would use on a D flute.

In the following pages I illustrate this third point with eight examples: tunes presented for the D flute earlier in this book which can *also* be played on keyless flutes in G, C or A (the three most useful non-D flutes).

Each of these eight tune transcriptions (listed on the next page) include:

- A sentence specifying which non-D flute to use (in italics, just below the tune title).
- The notes to play on that non-D flute, fingered *as if* you were playing them on a keyless D flute.
- Below that (in a box) the notes that are actually produced by using these fingerings on the specified non-D flute. As you will see, the tune comes out at the standard pitch level.
- Some thoughts on why you might want to use a non-D flute for that particular tune.

Non-D Flutes and Modal Scales

The following table represents flutes in six different keys and the eight modal scales that are easily playable, without half-holing or the use of keys, on each of these flutes.

Flute Key	Accessible Modal Scales (No Half-Holing Required)	
E	A Ionian (major) — 3 sharps E Mixolydian B Dorian F-sharp Aeolian (natural minor)	E Ionian (major) — 4 sharps B Mixolydian F-sharp Dorian C-sharp Aeolian (natural minor)
A	D Ionian (major) — 2 sharps A Mixolydian E Dorian B Aeolian (natural minor)	A Ionian (major) — 3 sharps E Mixolydian B Dorian F-sharp Aeolian (natural minor)
D	G Ionian (major) — 1 sharp D Mixolydian A Dorian E Aeolian (natural minor)	D Ionian (major) — 2 sharps A Mixolydian E Dorian B Aeolian (natural minor)
G	C Ionian (major) — no sharps or flats G Mixolydian D Dorian A Aeolian (natural minor)	G Ionian (major) — 1 sharp D Mixolydian A Dorian E Aeolian (natural minor)
C	F Ionian (major) — 1 flat C Mixolydian G Dorian D Aeolian (natural minor)	C Ionian (major) — no sharps or flats G Mixolydian D Dorian A Aeolian (natural minor)
F	B-flat Ionian (major) — 2 flats F Mixolydian C Dorian G Aeolian (natural minor)	F Ionian (major) — 1 flat C Mixolydian G Dorian D Aeolian (natural minor)

- The inner four rows of the table show the flutes that are most useful for Irish music (A, D, G and C).
- Note that the left (unshaded) group of scales in each row is identical to the right (shaded) group of scales in the row below it. This shows that each modal scale can be played on keyless flutes in two different keys.
- Each group of four scales shares a single mode signature. The number of sharps or flats in that mode signature is shown in the upper right corner of the cell.
- The order of the rows in the table follows the circle of fifths.

Another Reason to Try a Non-D Flute

Some tunes which can be played well on a keyless D flute can also be played, to very good effect and in the standard key, on a non-D flute. For two examples, see *The Orphan* and *Miss Patterson's Slipper* on pp. 121-123.

19th Century Non-D Flutes

In the 19th century a number of flute makers produced wooden simple-system flutes in B♭ (a major third lower than the D flute), E♭ (a half-step higher) and F (a minor third higher) for use in military bands. (Note that flutes pitched higher than D are sometimes referred to as "fifes.") These flutes are still used, in Northern Ireland and elsewhere, in Orange Lodge flute marching bands. These non-D flutes have often found their way into the hands of traditional players, providing them with fresh sounds to explore.

Simple-system piccolos were also popular among some Irish players, as evidenced by commercial recordings from early in the 20th century. These piccolos were usually pitched in D, an octave higher than the standard simple-system flute, or in a nearby key such as E♭ or F.

It was rare for 19th century flute makers to build wooden, simple-system flutes pitched lower than the low B♭, presumably due, in part, to the challenge of covering the six primary holes over such a large span.

Modern Non-D Flutes

Many players are drawn to the deep, sonorous tones of the low B♭ flute. A number of contemporary simple-system flute makers offer low flutes in B♭ based upon the 19th century instruments of the English flute making firm Rudall and Rose. Most players with average-size hands can readily handle these flutes. You can hear B♭ flutes in performances and on recordings by players such as Matt Molloy, Kevin Crawford and others. Typically, players use the same fingerings on the low B♭ that they would use on a D flute, thereby dropping the tune down in pitch by a major third.

At the time of this writing, excellent low A simple-system flutes are being made by flute makers Casey Burns, Chris Norman and perhaps others. I use a Burns low A to play the tunes you hear on CD #2, tracks 97-99 (see pp. 120-123). The Burns design makes the finger reach quite manageable for players with average-size hands. You may also play these tunes on a modern, Boehm-system alto flute, which is pitched the same as the simple-system low A.

Many flute makers offer low simple-system flutes in C, B and B♭ as well as flutes in a variety of keys higher than the standard D. You'll hear a Burns low C on CD #2, tracks 95 and 96 (see pp. 118-119) and a Burns high G on CD #2, tracks 92-94 (see pp. 114-117).

Low G flutes could be quite useful if they can be made to be manageable for players of Irish music. As of this writing, Chris Norman is the only flute maker I know of who is actively mounting this challenge.

The Tunes

The eight tunes in the Appendix appear twice on CD #2, played first on a D flute and later on a non-D flute. It is interesting to compare how D flute and non-D flute settings of the same tune can differ in terms of ornamentation options, tone colors, and changes in the register of notes or phrases.

Title	*Non-D Flute Setting*	*D Flute Setting*
Mullingar Lea (high G flute)	p. 114; CD 2, track 92	p. 107; CD 2, track 47
The Man From Glauntaun (high G flute)	p. 115; CD 2, track 93	p. 110; CD 2, track 54
Strop the Razor (high G flute)	p. 116; CD 2, track 94	p. 103; CD 2, track 37
The Maids of Mitchellstown (low C flute)	p. 118; CD 2, track 95	p. 105; CD 2, track 41
My Maryanne (low C flute)	p. 119; CD 2, track 96	p. 106; CD 2, track 44
Follow Me Down (low A flute)	p. 120; CD 2, track 97	p. 107; CD 2, track 48
The Orphan (low A flute)	p. 121; CD 2, track 98	p. 84; CD 2, track 1
Miss Patterson's Slipper (low A flute)	p. 122; CD 2, track 99	p. 89; CD 2, track 14

You'll find 28 more tunes that you can play on non-D flutes in the collection *150 Gems of Irish Music for Tin Whistle*, in the section called "Tunes for Non-D Whistles." A tune that fits well on a C whistle, for example, fits equally well on a flute in C.

Mullingar Lea · *Reel*

Play the following on a high G flute, fingered as if playing on a D flute.

CD 2, Track 92   For a D flute setting of this tune, refer to tune 141 on p. 107 and CD 2, track 47.

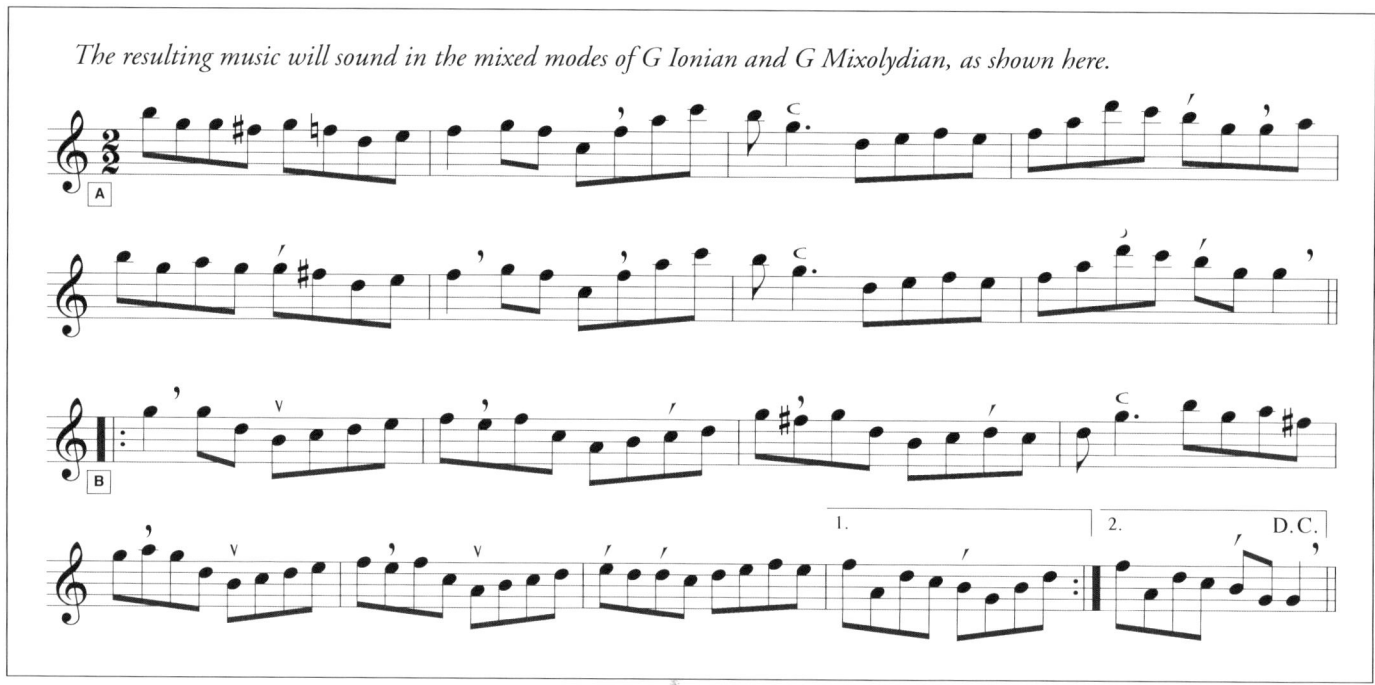

The resulting music will sound in the mixed modes of G Ionian and G Mixolydian, as shown here.

- It is difficult to play this tune on a keyless flute in D in the customary mixed modes of G Ionian and G Mixolydian due to the presence of F-naturals.
- It is much easier to accomplish this using a keyless flute in G.
- Played on a high G flute, the A-part sounds an octave higher than it does on most instruments, while the B-part sounds in unison with them. Certain notes in the B-part must be raised by an octave.
- To see and hear how most instruments play this tune, see tune 141 on p. 107 and listen to CD 2, track 47.
- A high G flute is one fourth higher than a D flute.
- On the G flute, you play this tune using fingerings that are one fifth *higher* (A-part) and one fourth *lower* (B-part) than those you would have to use on a keyless D flute. Such fingerings are much more flute-friendly.
- The music comes out sounding, as desired, in the mixed modes of G Ionian and G Mixolydian. Using a G flute in this way, you may play the tune along with all other instruments.

The Man From Glauntaun · *Slide*

Play the following on a high G flute, fingered as if playing on a D flute.

based on the playing of Dennis Doody (button accordion)
on the 1978 recording "Kerry Music"

CD 2, Track 93

For a D flute setting of this tune, refer to tune 148 on p. 110 and CD 2, track 54.

The resulting music will sound in the mixed modes of G Ionian and G Mixolydian, as shown here.

- It is difficult to play this tune on a keyless flute in D in the customary mixed modes of G Ionian and G Mixolydian due to the presence of F-naturals.
- It is much easier to accomplish this using a keyless flute in G.
- Played on a high G flute, the tune sounds in unison with most instruments.
- To see and hear how most instruments play this tune, see tune 148 on p. 110 and listen to CD 2, track 54.
- A high G flute is one fourth higher than a D flute.
- On the G flute, you play this tune using fingerings that are one fourth *lower* than those you would have to use on a keyless D flute. Such fingerings are much more flute-friendly.
- The music comes out sounding, as desired, in the mixed modes of G Ionian and G Mixolydian. Using a G flute in this way, you may play the tune along with all other instruments.

Strop the Razor · *Jig*

Play the following on a high G flute, fingered as if playing on a D flute.

CD 2, Track 94

For a D flute setting of this tune, refer to tune 131 on p. 103 and CD 2, track 37.

The resulting music will sound in the mixed modes of G Ionian and G Mixolydian, as shown here.

- It is difficult to play this tune on a keyless flute in D in the customary mixed modes of G Ionian and G Mixolydian due to the presence of F-naturals.
- It is much easier to accomplish this using a keyless flute in G.
- Played on a high G flute, the A-part and B-part sound an octave higher than they do on most instruments, while the C-part sounds in unison with them.
- To see and hear how most instruments play this tune, see tune 131 on p. 103 and listen to CD 2, track 37.
- A high G flute is one fourth higher than a D flute.
- On the G flute, you play this tune using fingerings that are one fifth *higher* (A-part and B-part) and one fourth *lower* (C-part) than those you would have to use on a keyless D flute. Such fingerings are much more flute-friendly.
- The music comes out sounding, as desired, in the mixed modes of G Ionian and G Mixolydian. Using a G flute in this way, you may play the tune along with all other instruments.

The Maids of Mitchellstown · *Reel*

Play the following on a C flute, fingered as if playing on a D flute.

CD 2, Track 95   For a D flute setting of this tune, refer to tune 135 on p. 105 and CD 2, track 41.

The resulting music will sound in D Dorian, as shown here.

- It is difficult to play this tune on a keyless flute in D in the customary mode of D Dorian due to the presence of F-naturals.
- It is much easier to accomplish this using a keyless flute in C.
- Played on a low C flute, the tune sounds in unison with most other instruments and you are able to play all the notes in their original register. (On most D flutes, you must raise by an octave the second to last note in the first ending of the A-part.)
- To see and hear how most instruments play this tune, see tune 135 on p. 105 and listen to CD 2, track 41.
- A low C flute is one whole step lower than a D flute.
- On the C flute, you play this tune using fingerings that are one whole step *higher* than those you would have to use on a keyless D flute. Such fingerings are much more flute-friendly.
- The music comes out sounding, as desired, in D Dorian. Using a C flute in this way, you may play the tune along with all other instruments.

My Maryanne · *Reel*

Play the following on a C flute, fingered as if playing on a D flute.

CD 2, Track 96   For a D flute setting of this tune, refer to tune 138 on p. 106 and CD 2, track 44.

The resulting music will sound in C Ionian, as shown here.

- It is difficult to play this tune on a keyless flute in D in the customary mode of C Ionian due to the presence of F-naturals.
- It is much easier to accomplish this using a keyless flute in C.
- Played on a low C flute, the tune sounds in unison with most instruments.
- To see and hear how most instruments play this tune, see tune 138 on p. 106 and listen to CD 2, track 44.
- A low C flute is one whole step lower than a D flute.
- On the C flute, you play this tune using fingerings that are one whole step *higher* than those you would have to use on a keyless D flute. Such fingerings are much more flute-friendly.
- The music comes out sounding, as desired, in C Ionian. Using a C flute in this way, you may play the tune along with all other instruments.

Follow Me Down · *Reel*

Play the following on a low A flute, fingered as if playing on a D flute.

based on the playing of Jackie Daly (button accordion) and Séamus Creagh (fiddle) on the 1977 recording "Jackie Daly Séamus Creagh"

CD 2, Track 97

For a D flute setting of this tune, refer to tune 142 on p. 107 and CD 2, track 48.

The resulting music will sound in B Dorian, as shown here.

- It is difficult to play this tune on a keyless flute in D in the customary mode of B Dorian due to the presence of G-sharps.
- It is much easier to accomplish this using a keyless flute in A, low or high.
- Played on a low A flute, the tune sounds in unison with most instruments for most of the A-part and an octave lower for the rest of the tune. On a high A flute, the tune would sound an octave higher than most instruments for most of the A-part and in unison with them for the rest of the tune.
- To see and hear how most instruments play this tune, see tune 142 on p. 107 and listen to CD 2, track 48.
- A low A flute is one fourth lower than a D flute.
- On an A flute, you play this tune using fingerings that are sometimes a fourth *higher* and sometimes a fifth *lower* than those you would have to use on a keyless D flute. Such fingerings are more flute-friendly.
- The music comes out sounding, as desired, in B Dorian. Using an A flute in this way, you may play the tune along with all other instruments.

The Orphan • *Jig*
Play the following on a low A flute, fingered as if playing on a D flute.

CD 2, Track 98   For a D flute setting of this tune, refer to tune 95 on p. 84 and CD 2, track 1.

- Playing this tune on a D flute, in the customary mode of E Dorian, puts it low in the flute's range, and some notes must be raised by an octave. Playing it on a low A flute lets you play all notes in their original register. (Playing on a high A flute would place the entire tune an octave higher than most other instruments play.)
- To see and hear how this tune may be played on a D flute, see tune 95 on p. 84 and listen to CD 2, track 1.
- Most other instruments play the tune with melodic contours like those shown in the box above.
- A low A flute is one fourth lower than a D flute.
- On an A flute (low or high), you play this tune using fingerings that are a fourth *higher* than those you would have to use on a keyless D flute.
- The music comes out sounding, as desired, in E Dorian. Using an A flute in this way, you may play the tune along with all other instruments.

Miss Patterson's Slipper · *Reel*

Play the following on a low A flute, fingered as if playing on a D flute.

CD 2, Track 99

For a D flute setting of this tune, refer to tune 108 on p. 89 and CD 2, track 14.

The resulting music will sound in E Dorian, as shown here.

- This tune has a wide range – just over two full octaves – and so is not often played on the flute. To do so, you must transpose a number of notes either up or down an octave. You can play the tune, in the customary mode of E Dorian, on either a D or an A flute. To see and hear how you might play this tune on a D flute, look at tune 108 on p. 89 and listen to CD 2, track 14.
- Using a low A flute, the A-part can be played without altering the register of any notes, while the B-part is mostly played an octave lower than usual. This makes for a dark, mellow sound overall, and the lovely melodic contours of the A-part are preserved. Also, most of the B-part sounds an octave below other melody instruments, lending depth and richness to the session sound.
- Using a high A flute, the A-part sounds an octave above most instruments, while most of the B-part sounds in unison with them.
- A low A flute is one fourth lower than a D flute. A high A flute is a fifth higher.
- On an A flute, you play this tune using fingerings that are a fourth *higher* (A-part) and a fifth *lower* (for most of the B-part) than those you would have to use on a keyless D flute.
- The music comes out sounding, as desired, in E Dorian. Using an A flute in this way, you may play the tune along with all other instruments.
- On the next page you may see how non-wind instruments would play this tune, and how the contours of that setting differ from the A flute version shown in the box above.

*Here is how most non-wind instruments would play the tune **Miss Patterson's Slipper**.*

Contents of the Companion Audio

Track number — *Page*

Audio #1

1. Have a Drink with Me — 48
2. Slieve Russell — 48
3. Hardiman's Fancy — 48
4. Breeches Mary — 49
5. Tenpenny Bit — 49
6. Fanning's Jig — 49
7. Thirsty for Drink — 50
8. The Humours of Glynn — 50
9. A Health to the Ladies — 51
10. Palm Sunday — 51
11. Sorry I Am — 51
12. The Humours of Trim — 52
13. The Lark on the Strand — 52
14. Munster Bacon — 52
15. Tell Her I Am (three-part version) — 53
16. Tell Her I Am (two-part version) — 53
17. A Tailor I Am — 54
18. The Wandering Minstrel — 54
19. Pullet Wants Cock — 55
20. Miller's Maggot — 55
21. My Love in the Morning — 55
22. Hudie Gallagher's March — 56
23. Down the Back Lane — 56
24. Tongs by the Fire — 57
25. Top of Cork Road — 57
26. I Ne'er Shall Wean Her — 57
27. The High Part of the Road — 58
28. Trip to Killavil — 58
29. Fraher's Jig — 58
30. Strike the Gay Harp — 59
31. Sword in Hand — 60
32. The Virginia Reel — 60
33. Sailing Into Walpole's Marsh — 60
34. The Queen of May — 61
35. Toss the Feathers — 61
36. The Earl's Chair — 61
37. The Chattering Magpie — 62
38. The Monaghan Twig — 62
39. Jackson's Reel — 62
40. The Maids of Mt. Kisco — 63
41. The Union Reel — 63
42. The Cameronian — 63
43. The Galway Rambler — 64
44. The Connaught Heifers — 64
45. The Longford Tinker — 64
46. The Green-Gowned Lass — 65
47. Boys on the Hilltop — 65
48. The Farewell Reel — 65
49. Fishermans' Lilt — 65
50. Killarney Boys of Pleasure — 66
51. The Corner House — 66
52. The Windy Gap — 66
53. The Reel with the Birl — 67
54. Ríl Phadaí 'n Atharaigh (Paddy From Agharagh) — 67
55. Lady Gordon — 67
56. Maud Miller — 68
57. The Crooked Road to Dublin — 68
58. Johnny Going to Céilí — 68
59. The Sailor's Bonnet — 68
60. The Colliers' Reel — 69
61. The Tap Room — 69
62. The Noisy Curlew — 69
63. The Ravelled Hank of Yarn — 70
64. Old Wheels of the World — 70
65. Sweeny's Dream — 70
66. The Connemara Stocking — 70
67. Mary McMahon — 71
68. Drogheda Bay — 71
69. Miss Monaghan — 71
70. The Old High Reel — 72
71. McDonagh's — 72
72. George White's Favorite — 72
73. O'Callaghan's — 73
74. The Blackbird (hornpipe) — 73
75. Boys of Ballycastle — 73
76. The First of May — 74
77. Kit O'Mahoney's — 74
78. The Brown Chest — 74
79. Poll Ha'penny — 75
80. The Five Roads — 75
81. The Pleasures of Hope — 75
82. Fitzgerald's — 76
83. Tuamgraney Castle — 76
84. I'm the Boy for Bewitching Them — 77
85. The Ship Doctor — 77
86. My Mind Will Never Be Easy — 77
87. Ballydesmond Polka #1 — 77
88. Din Tarrant's — 78
89. Pádraig O'Keeffe's — 78
90. Get Up Old Woman and Shake Yourself — 78
91. Martin Kirwan's March — 79
92. The Blackbird (set dance) — 79
93. George Brabazon — 79
94. Lord Inchiquin — 80

Audio #2

1. The Orphan — 84
2. The Cordal Jig — 84
3. Paddy's Resource — 84
4. Vincent Campbell's — 85
5. Bush on the Hill — 85
6. Haste to the Wedding — 86
7. Jack Walsh's Jig — 86
8. Child of My Heart — 86
9. The Gold Ring — 87
10. The Humours of Loughrea — 88
11. Down the Broom — 88
12. Fred Finn's — 88
13. Music in the Glen — 89
14. Miss Patterson's Slipper — 89
15. The Galtee Reel — 89

16. Miss McLeod's Reel	90
17. The Duke of Leinster	90
18. Dr. Gilbert	91
19. Hand Me Down the Tackle	91
20. The Humours of Lissadell	91
21. The Green Hills of Tyrol	92
22. Kitty's Wedding	93
23. Jack O'Neill's Fancy	93
24. The Pride of Petravore	93
25. Madam If You Please	94
26. Blackwater Polka #2	95
27. O'Connell's Farewell to Dublin	95
28. An Cúisín Bán (The White Cushion)	95
29. The Hag's Purse	100
30. An Buachaill Dreoite (The Spent Boy)	100
31. The Banks of Glenloe	100
32. The Gallowglass	101
33. The Luck Penny	101
34. Wellington's Advance	102
35. The Dance by the Old Sally Tree	102
36. The Cauliflower Jig	102
37. Strop the Razor	103
38. The Chicago Reel	104
39. Castle Kelly	104
40. McFadden's Handsome Daughter	104
41. The Maids of Mitchellstown	105
42. The Girl That Broke My Heart	105
43. The Humours of Scariff	105
44. My Maryanne	106
45. The Big Reel of Ballynacally	106
46. The Tempest	106
47. Mullingar Lea	107
48. Follow Me Down	107
49. Bunch of Green Rushes	107
50. The New Century	108
51. Chief O'Neill's Favorite	108
52. The Ebb Tide	108
53. Early in the Morning	109
54. The Man From Glauntaun	110
55. John Doherty's Mazurka	110
56. Down the Hill	111
57. Figure 6	16
58. Figure 9	18
59. Figure 12	19
60. Figures 16 and 19	21, 22
61. Figure 22	23
62. Figures 24 and 25	23
63. Figures 26 and 27	25
64. Figure 29	25
65. Figure 30	26
66. Figure 32	27
67. Figure 33	28
68. Figure 34	29
69. Figure 35	30
70. Figure 36	30
71. Figure 38	37
72. Figure 39	37
73. Figure 40	37
74. Figure 41	37
75. Figure 42	38
76. Figure 43	38
77. Figure 44	38
78. Figure 46	39
79. Figure 47	39
80. Figure 48	39
81. Figure 49	39
82. Figure 50	40
83. Figure 52	40
84. Figure 54	41
85. Figure 56	41
86. Figure 58	42
87. Figure 59	42
88. Figure 60	42
89. Figure 62	43
90. Figure 63	43
91. Figure 64	43
92. Mullingar Lea (high G flute)	114
93. The Man From Glauntaun (high G flute)	115
94. Strop the Razor (high G flute)	116
95. The Maids of Mitchellstown (low C flute)	118
96. My Maryanne (low C flute)	119
97. Follow Me Down (low A flute)	120
98. The Orphan (low A flute)	121
99. Miss Patterson's Slipper (low A flute)	122

The ornamentation shown in the transcriptions is reflected in the audio recordings for the first time through each part of the tune. During the repetition of any part, the ornamentation heard on the recording may vary in small ways from what is written.

The breath marks shown in the transcriptions represent breathing opportunities, not required breathing places. On the recording, I used only the breathing opportunities I needed at that time. In most cases, using all of the indicated breathing opportunities would result in music that sounds too fragmented. For more on this subject, see p. 36.

On all of Audio #1, and on tracks 1-91 of Audio #2, I played a wooden flute made by Firth, Pond & Company, New York City, c. 1848- 1863, with a wooden headjoint made by Chris Abell in Asheville, North Carolina in 2012.

On tracks 92-99 of Audio #2, I played wooden flutes by Casey Burns in high G, low C and low A, all made in Kingston, Washington between 2003 and 2013.

Index of Tune Titles

An Buachaill Dreoite	100
An Cúisín Bán	95
Ballydesmond Polka #1	77
Banks of Glenloe, The	100
Big Reel of Ballynacally, The	106
Blackbird, The (hornpipe)	73
Blackbird, The (set dance)	79
Blackwater Polka #2	95
Boys of Ballycastle	73
Boys on the Hilltop	65
Breeches Mary	49
Brown Chest, The	74
Bunch of Green Rushes	107
Bush on the Hill	85
Cameronian, The	63
Castle Kelly	104
Cauliflower Jig, The	102
Chattering Magpie, The	62
Chicago Reel, The	104
Chief O'Neill's Favorite	108
Child of My Heart	86
Colliers' Reel, The	69
Connaught Heifers, The	64
Connemara Stocking, The	70
Cordal Jig, The	84
Corner House, The	66
Crooked Road to Dublin, The	68
Dance by the Old Sally Tree, The	102
Din Tarrant's	78
Down the Back Lane	56
Down the Broom	88
Down the Hill	111
Dr. Gilbert	91
Drogheda Bay	71
Duke of Leinster, The	90
Earl's Chair, The	61
Early in the Morning	109
Ebb Tide, The	108
Fanning's Jig	49
Farewell Reel, The	65
First of May, The	74
Fisherman's Lilt	65
Fitzgerald's	76
Five Roads, The	75
Follow Me Down	107, 120
Fraher's Jig	58
Fred Finn's	88
Gallowglass, The	101
Galtee Reel, The	89
Galway Rambler, The	64
George Brabazon	79
George White's Favorite	72
Get Up Old Woman and Shake Yourself	78
Girl That Broke My Heart, The	105
Gold Ring, The	87
Green Hills of Tyrol, The	92
Green-Gowned Lass, The	65
Hag's Purse, The	100
Hand Me Down the Tackle	91
Hardiman's Fancy	48
Haste to the Wedding	86
Have a Drink with Me	48
Health to the Ladies, A	51
High Part of the Road, The	58
Hudie Gallagher's March	56
Humours of Glynn, The	50
Humours of Lissadell, The	91
Humours of Loughrea, The	88
Humours of Scariff, The	105
Humours of Trim, The	52
I Ne'er Shall Wean Her	57
I'm the Boy for Bewitching Them	77
Jack O'Neill's Fancy	93
Jack Walsh's Jig	86
Jackson's Reel	62
John Doherty's Mazurka	110
Johnny Going to Céilí	68
Killarney Boys of Pleasure	66
Kit O'Mahoney's	74
Kitty's Wedding	93
Lady Gordon	67
Lark on the Strand, The	52
Longford Tinker, The	64
Lord Inchiquin	80
Luck Penny, The	101
Madam If You Please	94
Maids of Mitchellstown, The	105, 118
Maids of Mt. Kisco, The	63
Man From Glauntaun, The	110, 115
Martin Kirwan's March	79
Mary McMahon	71
Maud Miller	68
McDonagh's	72
McFadden's Handsome Daughter	104
Miller's Maggot	55
Miss McLeod's Reel	90
Miss Monaghan	71
Miss Patterson's Slipper	89, 122
Monaghan Twig, The	62
Mullingar Lea	107, 114
Munster Bacon	52
Music in the Glen	89
My Love in the Morning	55
My Maryanne	106, 119
My Mind Will Never Be Easy	77
New Century, The	108
Noisy Curlew, The	69
O'Callaghan's	73
O'Connell's Farewell to Dublin	95
Old High Reel, The	72
Old Wheels of the World	70
Orphan, The	84, 121
Paddy From Agharagh	67
Paddy's Resource	84
Palm Sunday	51
Pádraig O'Keeffe's	78
Pleasures of Hope, The	75
Poll Ha'penny	75
Pride of Petravore, The	93
Pullet Wants Cock	55
Queen of May, The	61
Ravelled Hank of Yarn, The	70
Reel with the Birl, The	67
Ríl Phadaí 'n Atharaigh	67
Sailing into Walpole's Marsh	60
Sailor's Bonnet, The	68
Ship Doctor, The	77
Slieve Russell	48
Sorry I Am	51
Spent Boy, The	100
Strike the Gay Harp	59
Strop the Razor	103, 116
Sweeny's Dream	70
Sword in Hand	60
Tailor I Am, A	54
Tap Room, The	69
Tell Her I Am (three-part version)	53
Tell Her I Am (two-part version)	53
Tempest, The	106
Tenpenny Bit	49
Thirsty for Drink	50
Tongs by the Fire	57
Top of Cork Road	57
Toss the Feathers	61
Trip to Killavil	58
Tuamgraney Castle	76
Union Reel, The	63
Vincent Campbell's	85
Virginia Reel, The	60
Wandering Minstrel, The	54
Wellington's Advance	102
White Cushion, The	95
Windy Gap, The	66

Index of Tunes by Tune Type

JIGS

An Buachaill Dreoite	100
Banks of Glenloe, The	100
Breeches Mary	49
Bush on the Hill	85
Cauliflower Jig, The	102
Child of My Heart	86
Cordal Jig, The	84
Dance by the Old Sally Tree, The	102
Down the Back Lane	56
Fanning's Jig	49
Fraher's Jig	58
Gallowglass, The	101
Gold Ring, The	87
Hag's Purse, The	100
Hardiman's Fancy	48
Haste to the Wedding	86
Have a Drink with Me	48
Health to the Ladies, A	51
High Part of the Road, The	58
Hudie Gallagher's March	56
Humours of Glynn, The	50
Humours of Trim, The	52
I Ne'er Shall Wean Her	57
Jack Walsh's Jig	86
Lark on the Strand, The	52
Luck Penny, The	101
Miller's Maggot	55
Munster Bacon	52
My Love in the Morning	55
Orphan, The	84, 121
Paddy's Resource	84
Palm Sunday	51
Pullet Wants Cock	55
Slieve Russell	48
Sorry I Am	51
Spent Boy, The	100
Strike the Gay Harp	59
Strop the Razor	103, 116
Tailor I Am, A	54
Tell Her I Am (three-part version)	53
Tell Her I Am (two-part version)	53
Tenpenny Bit	49
Thirsty for Drink	50
Tongs by the Fire	57
Top of Cork Road	57
Trip to Killavil	58
Vincent Campbell's	85
Wandering Minstrel, The	54
Wellington's Advance	102

REELS

Big Reel of Ballynacally, The	106
Boys on the Hilltop	65
Bunch of Green Rushes	107
Cameronian, The	63
Castle Kelly	104
Chattering Magpie, The	62
Chicago Reel, The	104
Colliers' Reel, The	69
Connaught Heifers, The	64
Connemara Stocking, The	70
Corner House, The	66
Crooked Road to Dublin, The	68
Down the Broom	88
Dr. Gilbert	91
Drogheda Bay	71
Duke of Leinster, The	90
Earl's Chair, The	61
Farewell Reel, The	65
Fisherman's Lilt	65
Follow Me Down	107, 120
Fred Finn's	88
Galtee Reel, The	89
Galway Rambler, The	64
George White's Favorite	72
Girl That Broke My Heart, The	105
Green Hills of Tyrol, The	92
Green-Gowned Lass, The	65
Hand Me Down the Tackle	91
Humours of Lissadell, The	91
Humours of Loughrea, The	88
Humours of Scariff, The	105
Jackson's Reel	62
Johnny Going to Céilí	68
Killarney Boys of Pleasure	66
Lady Gordon	67
Longford Tinker, The	64
Maids of Mitchellstown, The	105, 118
Maids of Mt. Kisco, The	63
Mary McMahon	71
Maud Miller	68
McDonagh's	72
McFadden's Handsome Daughter	104
Miss McLeod's Reel	90
Miss Monaghan	71
Miss Patterson's Slipper	89, 122
Monaghan Twig, The	62
Mullingar Lea	107, 114
Music in the Glen	89
My Maryanne	106, 119
Noisy Curlew, The	69
Old High Reel, The	72
Old Wheels of the World	70
Paddy From Agharagh	67
Queen of May, The	61
Ravelled Hank of Yarn, The	70
Reel with the Birl, The	67
Ríl Phadaí 'n Atharaigh	67
Sailing into Walpole's Marsh	60
Sailor's Bonnet, The	68
Sweeny's Dream	70
Sword in Hand	60
Tap Room, The	69
Tempest, The	106
Toss the Feathers	61
Union Reel, The	63
Virginia Reel, The	60
Windy Gap, The	66

HORNPIPES

Blackbird, The	73
Boys of Ballycastle	73
Brown Chest, The	74
Chief O'Neill's Favorite	108
Early in the Morning	109
Ebb Tide, The	108
First of May, The	74
Fitzgerald's	76
Five Roads, The	75
Jack O'Neill's Fancy	93
Kit O'Mahoney's	74
Kitty's Wedding	93
Madam If You Please	94
New Century, The	108
O'Callaghan's	73
Pleasures of Hope, The	75
Poll Ha'penny	75
Pride of Petravore, The	93
Tuamgraney Castle	76

POLKAS

Ballydesmond Polka #1	77
Blackwater Polka #2	95
Din Tarrant's	78

SLIDES

Get Up Old Woman and Shake Yourself	78
Man From Glauntaun, The	110, 115
O'Connell's Farewell to Dublin	95
Pádraig O'Keeffe's	78

SLIP JIGS & HOP JIGS

I'm the Boy for Bewitching Them	77
My Mind Will Never Be Easy	77
Ship Doctor, The	77

SET DANCES

An Cúisín Bán	95
Blackbird, The	79
O'Connell's Farewell to Dublin	95
White Cushion, The	95

HARP PIECES

George Brabazon	79
Lord Inchiquin	80

OTHER

Down the Hill	111
John Doherty's Mazurka	110
Martin Kirwan's March	79

Index of Tune Sources

Approximately one third of the transcriptions in this collection are based on the playing of specific musicians and groups. They are listed below.

In most cases, I based the transcription on a commercial or field recording. Information on the recording is given with the transcription.

In other cases, the transcription is based on my memory of the tune as I learned it by ear from the musician or musicians in question.

Musician or Group	Page
Altan (group)	110
Bergin, Mary (tin whistle)	63
Bothy Band (group)	64
Brady, Paul (guitar)	60
Burke, Kevin (fiddle)	60, 64
Byrne, Dermot (button accordion)	110
Byrne, Francie (fiddle)	56, 67
Byrne, Mickey (fiddle)	56, 67
Byrne, Tom (flute)	55, 65, 74
Canny, Paddy (fiddle)	56, 69, 101
Casey, Bobby (fiddle)	70, 75
Chulrua (group)	102
Creagh, Séamus (fiddle)	107, 120
Crehan, Terry (fiddle)	104
Cronin, Paddy (fiddle)	76, 93
Daly, Jackie (button accordion)	107, 120
Doody, Dennis (button accordion)	78, 95, 110, 115
Farr, Lucy (fiddle)	79
Irvine, Andy (bouzouki)	60
Keane, Seán (fiddle)	85
Keenan, Paddy (uilleann pipes)	64
Kelly, John (concertina)	108
Kelly, Patrick (fiddle)	95
Kennedy, Frankie (flute)	110
Kennedy, Michael J. (melodeon in G)	51, 86, 90
McCaffrey, Tom (fiddle)	55, 65, 74
Molloy, Matt (flute)	64, 71, 85, 104
Moloney, Eddie (flute)	50
Mulcahy Family (group)	100
Mulcahy, Louise (uilleann pipes)	100
Mulcahy, Michelle (concertina)	100
Mulcahy, Mick (concertina)	100
Murphy, Dennis (fiddle)	49, 78
Ní Mhaonaigh, Mairéad (fiddle)	110
O'Brien, Paddy (button accordion)	102
O'Connell, Connie (fiddle)	53, 54
Ourceau, Patrick (fiddle)	67, 74, 91, 102
Ó hAllmhuráin, Gearóid (concertina)	67, 74, 91
Ó Riada, Peadar (concertina)	53, 54

About the Author

Grey Larsen was born in 1955 in New York City. His family moved to Cincinnati, Ohio the following year. Beginning piano lessons at the age of four, he enjoyed a childhood and youth full of musical exploration, his inner world filled with the keyboard music of Bach and Mozart, as well as the early rock, R&B and Motown sounds on the radio, the songs of contemporary folk music interpreters and traditional Appalachian and Irish music.

From 1970 to 1972 he studied at the Cincinnati College–Conservatory of Music before moving on, in 1973, to continue at the Oberlin Conservatory of Music in Oberlin, Ohio. While pursuing early music and composition on the one hand, he came ever more deeply under the spell of traditional music on the other, and for several years he followed these parallel streams with equal energy and dedication. In these and later years, he spent a great deal of time (in Cincinnati and Cleveland, Ohio) learning traditional Irish music from elder Irish immigrant musicians, most notably Co. Galway melodeon player Michael J. Kennedy (1900–1978), Co. Sligo flute player Tom Byrne (1920–2001) and Co. Leitrim fiddler Tom McCaffrey (1916-2006).

Upon completing a Bachelor of Music degree at Oberlin in 1976, the streams diverged. He bid a fond farewell to his academic path and set a course following his love of traditional music, exploring musical waterways that would branch, cross and rejoin over the decades.

He leads a varied and rich musical life in Bloomington, Indiana as a performer, teacher, author, recording artist, record producer, mastering engineer and music editor. Since the early 1970s he has also devoted himself to the traditional fiddle music of his native Midwest and Appalachia, in particular the music of southern Indiana fiddler Joe Dawson.

Books and Recordings by Grey Larsen

BOOKS

The Essential Guide to Irish Flute and Tin Whistle
The Essential Tin Whistle Toolbox
150 Gems of Irish Music for Flute
150 Gems of Irish Music for Tin Whistle
300 Gems of Irish Music for All Instruments
Down the Back Lane: Variation in Traditional Irish Dance Music
The Toolbox Tune Collection
The Toolbox Exercises for Finger Coordination
The Lotus Dickey Songbook
    (with Nancy C. McEntire and Janne Henshaw)

Most of these books include companion audio.

More information is available at www.greylarsen.com.

SELECTED RECORDINGS

with Cindy Kallet
    Cross the Water
    Back When We Were All Machines

with André Marchand
    The Orange Tree
    Les Marionnettes

with Paddy League
    The Green House
    Dark of the Moon

with Metamora
    Metamora
    The Great Road
    Morning Walk

with Malcolm Dalglish
    Banish Misfortune
    The First of Autumn
    Thunderhead

solo (with friends)
    The Gathering

Notes

Notes